D0201656

LINGUISTICALLY APPROPRIATE PRACTICE

A Guide for Working with Young Immigrant Children

Roma Chumak-Horbatsch

UNIVERSITY OF TORONTO PRESS

Copyright © University of Toronto Press Incorporated 2012
Higher Education Division

www.utppublishing.com

All rights reserved. The use of any part of this publication reproduced, transmitted in any form or by any means, electronic, mechanical, photocopying, recording, or otherwise, or stored in a retrieval system, without prior written consent of the publisher—or in the case of photocopying, a licence from Access Copyright (Canadian Copyright Licensing Agency), One Yonge Street, Suite 1900, Toronto, Ontario M5E 1E5—is an infringement of the copyright law.

Library and Archives Canada Cataloguing in Publication

Chumak-Horbatsch, Roma, 1947–

    Linguistically appropriate practice : a guide for working with young immigrant children / Roma Chumak-Horbatsch.

Includes bibliographical references and index.
Issued also in electronic formats.
ISBN 978-1-4426-0380-6

    1. Immigrant children—Education (Early childhood). 2. Education, Bilingual. 3. Multilingual education. 4. Language and education.   I. Title.

LC3715.C49 2012   370.117'5   C2012-905178-0

We welcome comments and suggestions regarding any aspect of our publications—please feel free to contact us at news@utphighereducation.com or visit our Internet site at www.utppublishing.com.

North America
5201 Dufferin Street
North York, Ontario, Canada, M3H 5T8

2250 Military Road
Tonawanda, New York, USA, 14150

ORDERS PHONE: 1–800–565–9523
ORDERS FAX: 1–800–221–9985
ORDERS E-MAIL: utpbooks@utpress.utoronto.ca

UK, Ireland, and continental Europe
NBN International
Estover Road, Plymouth, PL6 7PY, UK
ORDERS PHONE: 44 (0) 1752 202301
ORDERS FAX: 44 (0) 1752 202333
ORDERS E-MAIL: enquiries@nbninternational.com

This book is printed on paper containing 100% post-consumer fibre.

The University of Toronto Press acknowledges the financial support for its publishing activities of the Government of Canada through the Canada Book Fund.

Typesetting: Em Dash Design

Printed in Canada

RECYCLED
Paper made from
recycled material
FSC® C103567

To Marko

LINGUISTICALLY APPROPRIATE PRACTICE

CALGARY PUBLIC LIBRARY

MAR   2013

CONTENTS

FOREWORD

I read Roma Chumak-Horbatsch's book *Linguistically Appropriate Practice* with increasing excitement. As the pages turned, the future linguistic landscape of Canada began to change before my eyes. A detailed roadmap was being provided for enlightened and imaginative early childhood education, steering us away from the massive squandering of Canada's rich linguistic resources that has been characteristic of our educational practice since the beginnings of formal schooling.

Few would deny that Canada's cities are vibrant multilingual and multicultural environments; yet these same cities are *linguistic graveyards* for the home languages of countless children. Far too many children enter preschool programs or Junior Kindergarten fluent in their home languages only to have this fluency undermined by the intentional or inadvertent messages they receive in these environments. They quickly intuit that only one language is legitimate in the institutions of the wider society, and it's not their home language (Cummins, 1991; Sirén, 1991; Wong Fillmore, 1991). In far too many homes, a language gap opens up between children and parents; and this gap all too frequently becomes a chasm between children and their grandparents who may know minimal English or French.

The pattern of language loss can be illustrated in a longitudinal study of Portuguese home language use by children in the Toronto area (Cummins, 1991). Children were followed for three years, from age 4 through 6 (Junior Kindergarten through Grade 1). Detailed interview assessments with the children showed that by the time they had completed Grade 1, only 2 (out of 14) were rated as more conversationally proficient in Portuguese than in English, and only 3 were rated as equally proficient in each language. It is interesting to note that those children who were maintaining Portuguese were also developing significantly stronger English reading skills. Although the numbers of students in the study are small, there were extremely large differences (one standard deviation, equivalent to about 15 IQ-score-type points) in English reading skills in favour of children who were maintaining Portuguese language skills (N=6, ratings of 3–5 on Portuguese oral proficiency) as compared to those who were losing the language (N=8, ratings of 1–2 on Portuguese oral proficiency).

As Roma Chumak-Horbatsch points out, practice during the past decade or so has shifted away from overtly assimilative or "Anglo-conformity" orientations where children were routinely reprimanded for speaking their home languages within the school or preschool. Parents are no longer being advised that they should switch to English (or French in Quebec) in speaking with their children if they want them to succeed academically (although this practice appears still to linger among psychologists working in medical environments). In Ontario and other provinces, Ministry of Education curriculum documents are increasingly communicating a positive orientation toward the maintenance of children's home languages (e.g., Ontario Ministry of Education, 2006).

Thus, there has been a shift to what Chumak-Horbatsch calls a "supportive" approach to children's home languages and cultures. This approach "recognizes and values cultural and linguistic differences, acknowledges the importance of home languages, and supports immigrant children as they navigate and reconcile their two cultures" (Chapter 3, p. 2–3, ms). Yet, despite its good intentions, the supportive approach remains locked in monolingual practices that fail to address in a sufficiently positive way the dual language realities of emergent bilingual children. This can be illustrated by the account of one Grade 4 child in the Toronto area who was reflecting on when and where it was appropriate to use her two languages: "I am not always comfortable speaking Cantonese when I have to go to the office for some reason. I don't like it because a lot of teachers are at the office, and I don't like speaking it in front of them. I know that they are listening to me. I get nervous and afraid. For example, once I didn't feel very well in Grade 1. So my teacher sent me to the office to call my grandma. My grandma doesn't speak English, and she also can't hear very well, so I had to speak in Cantonese very loudly for her to hear. So when I spoke to my grandma, I felt very nervous."

In this example, it is highly unlikely that the student would have been reprimanded for speaking Cantonese in calling home (the school saw itself as very much an intercultural environment). However, she has internalized the sense that school is an English-only zone and no other language is legitimate within this space. Despite its supportive intercultural orientation, the school has not been sufficiently proactive in challenging the devaluation of marginalized languages and cultures in the society at large. Under these circumstances the school/preschool remains complicit with the power relations operating in the society at large.

But surely there is a practical issue here—how can teachers promote children's knowledge of and pride in their home languages when their classrooms are essentially mini–United Nations, characterized by multiple languages that may shift from year to year? Herein lies the genius of the inclusive pedagogies outlined in *Linguistically Appropriate Practice*. The detailed strategies and lesson plans contained in this book were conceived by working directly with multilingual children, taking account of what we know about bilingual language use ("translanguaging"), and drawing on initiatives that have proved successful in other contexts (e.g., the United Kingdom). All are eminently practical and easy to implement, and all communicate to children and parents the inestimable value of maintaining and developing children's home languages.

The practical nature of the pedagogical strategies incorporated within the construct of *Linguistically Appropriate Practice* removes any claim that this approach is not feasible in view of the diversity of languages and cultures in our schools and preschools. Educators and policymakers thus have the choice to either move in this direction or maintain the status quo. What arguments are there for maintaining the status quo?

- Can one reasonably claim that language loss is not a reality for the majority of Canadian-born emergent bilingual students? Obviously not—the data are abundantly clear that monolingual preschool and school programs contribute to children's language loss.
- Can one reasonably claim that promotion of children's home language development will confuse them and interfere with their acquisition of English or French and future academic success? Obviously not—as outlined in this book, the research data are clear in pointing to bilingualism as a positive force in children's cognitive and linguistic development.
- Can one reasonably claim that time devoted to linguistically appropriate practice would be better spent promoting children's skills in the dominant language? Again, the research data are clear that conceptual and academic skills transfer across languages, and time devoted to minority language instruction entails no adverse effects on children's development of academic skills in the majority language. In fact, the trends over time are for positive relationships between home language promotion within the school and development of academic skills in the majority language. Students who develop literacy skills in their home languages tend to perform

better on measures of literacy skills in the majority language (August & Shanahan, 2006).

In short, resistance to linguistically appropriate practice is likely to be rooted in ideological concerns rather than in any reasoned argument related to child development. Ideologies are not in any way inherently problematic. For example, this book is rooted in an ideology that children's linguistic, cultural, and intellectual talents should be affirmed in all their interactions with educators. The ideologies that underlie assimilative approaches to education are clearly at variance with this inclusive orientation.

My hope is that this book will bring these ideological issues to the forefront of debate so that their merits can be rationally discussed and evaluated. Ideologies are at their most insidious when they lurk unacknowledged and unrecognized in policies, educational practices, and assessment instruments. For example, the Early Development Index (EDI; Janus & Offord, 2000) has been widely used to judge the quality of children's cognitive, emotional, and linguistic development in the early years and also to assess the impact of intervention programs (e.g., McCain, Mustard, & Shankar, 2007; Pascal, 2009). Yet this instrument focuses only on children's language development in *English* (or other dominant languages in different societies), ignoring the impact that home use of other languages might have on the accuracy of assessment. In a context such as the Greater Toronto Area where approximately 50 per cent of children use a language other than English at home, this omission is neither accidental nor intentional. Rather it constitutes an example of willful blindness to issues that are not visible through the dominant policy lens, which is monolingual in focus.

Ideology in the form of willful blindness is also at play in the failure to acknowledge the relevance of linguistic diversity for policy in recent influential (and important) reports on early childhood education in Ontario (McCain & Mustard, 1999; McCain, Mustard, & Shankar, 2007; Pascal, 2009). Consider the following passage from the McCain, Mustard, and Shankar (2007) report: "Individuals who develop an understanding of two languages early in life have denser grey matter in the left hemisphere of the brain than individuals with monolingual backgrounds. They find it easier to learn third and fourth languages later in life. Neurons in the auditory cortex that respond to sound develop a sensitivity to the sounds of different languages in early life that make it easier to differentiate the sounds and develop the neurological pathways necessary for capability with multiple languages.... A recent study suggests that bilingualism from infancy, if sustained, can significantly inhibit the onset of dementia in the late years of life" (pp. 25–26).

Unfortunately, the authors fail to acknowledge that current monolingually oriented early childhood policies inadvertently contribute to ensuring that children's bilingualism will *not* be sustained for very long into elementary school. They also make no recommendations regarding early childhood policies and practices that might support children and parents in nurturing their linguistic advantages. Fortunately, *Linguistically Appropriate Practice* fills this gaping hole in current policy discourses in Ontario and beyond.

There is a danger that *Linguistically Appropriate Practice* might short-change itself as a result of the focus on "language" in its title. What we are talking about is *educationally appropriate practice*. This point was brought home to me personally in the late 1970s when I was just beginning to think about these issues. The occasion was the closing keynote speech delivered by Professor Mary Ashworth of the University of British Colombia at a conference on Teaching English as a Second Language (TESL) in Toronto. Mary concluded her speech by making the point that many students come to school either already bilingual in their home language and English or in the process of becoming bilingual. However, 12 years later, a large proportion of these students leave school monolingual in English (or French in Quebec). Mary pointed out that education is supposed to make children *more* than they were, but, in the case of bilingual children, it was often making them *less* than they were. The very essence of the term *education*—the nurturing of students' abilities and talents— was being negated by the education they were receiving in Canadian schools.

For me, this was a startling and disturbing insight. Clearly, in contexts characterized by racism or other forms of overt discrimination, schools have systematically reinforced the coercive power relations of the wider society. However, Mary was talking about the *Canadian* educational system, which, at that time, was busy wrapping itself in the cloak of multiculturalism. The idea that Canadian schools and educators could be agents in the reduction of students' potential and the constriction of possibilities—whether inadvertently or intentionally—was provocative.

However, Mary's point was that, as educators, we have the power to challenge these discriminatory structures and discourses and expand rather than constrict students' identity options. The title of her book *Blessed with Bilingual Brains* expressed this point very clearly (Ashworth, 1988).

In the same way, *Linguistically Appropriate Practice* provides educators with choices. It asks us to define our educational goals as we work with children over a period of months or years. Our educational goals will determine what constitutes educationally appropriate practice for us as educators. If our educational goals focus narrowly only on intellectual accomplishments that can be expressed through the dominant language, then we will choose to follow the well-trodden path of current practice that risks contributing to the loss of children's linguistic and educational potential. However, if our educational goals include affirming children's linguistic, cultural, and intellectual talents and accomplishments, then we will choose the directions clearly mapped by *Linguistically Appropriate Practice* in order to augment what children bring to school. In so doing, we will simultaneously augment the linguistic intelligence of our society and transform the landscape of what schools and preschools can achieve.

Jim Cummins

Toronto

References

Ashworth, M. (1988). *Blessed with bilingual brains.* Vancouver: Pacific Educational Press, University of British Columbia.

August, D., & Shanahan, T. (Eds.) (2006). *Developing literacy in second-language learners. Report of the National Literacy Panel on language-minority children and youth.* Mahwah, NJ: Lawrence Erlbaum Associates.

Cummins, J. (1991). The development of bilingual proficiency from home to school: A longitudinal study of Portuguese-speaking children. *Journal of Education*, 173(2), 85–98.

Janus, M., & Offord, D. (2000). Readiness to learn at school. *ISUMA Canadian Journal of Policy Research*, 1(2), 71–75.

McCain, M.N., & Mustard, F. (1999). *Reversing the brain drain: Early years study: Final report.* Toronto: Ontario Children's Secretariat.

McCain, M., Mustard, F., & Shanker, S. (2007). *Early Years Study 2: Putting science into action.* Toronto: Council for Early Child Development.

Ontario Ministry of Education (2006). *Many roots, many voices. Supporting English language learners in every classroom: A practical guide for Ontario educators.* Toronto: Ministry of Education, Ontario.

Pascal, C.E. (2009, June). *With our best future in mind: Implementing early learning in Ontario. Report to the Premier by the Special Advisor on Early Learning.* Toronto: Queen's Printer. Retrieved from http://www.ontario.ca/ontprodconsume/ groups/content/@onca/@initiatives/documents/document/onto6_018899.pdf.

Sirén, U. (1991). *Minority language transmission in early childhood: Parental intention and language use.* Stockholm: Institute of International Education, Stockholm University.

Wong Fillmore, L. (1991). When learning a second language means losing the first. *Early Childhood Research Quarterly*, 6, 323–346.

ACKNOWLEDGEMENTS

I would like to express my gratitude to all those who helped in the preparation of this book. My biggest thanks go to the children! The remarkable, at times moving experiences I had with them showed me a new face of bilingualism. I am also grateful to the many parents who helped me understand the bilingual hopes they have for their children.

A very special thanks to Dr. Jim Cummins who was always generous with his time, provided sound guidance and advice, and helped me as I travelled from idea to proposal to book. A heartfelt thanks to Monique Bélanger, editor, consultant, word detective, table creator, file organizer, and friend. Her careful attention to my work, her many wise suggestions and sense of humour were a tremendous support as I prepared this book. Merci, Monique!

I thank all the practitioners and students who shared their experiences, stories, and anecdotes with me. Special thanks to the Ryerson University Early Learning Centre team, who eagerly and enthusiastically embraced LAP, and made it their own.

A warm thank you to my research assistant, Laura Petrenko, who completed task after task with enthusiasm, diligence, and thoroughness. I would also like to express my thanks to the people who took the time to review a draft of this book. Thank you also to Anne Brackenbury and the team at the Higher Education Division, University of Toronto Press.

Finally, I would also like to express my deepest affection and gratitude to my husband Marko, for his encouragement and never-ending support. It is to him that I dedicate this book.

THE ROAD TO LINGUISTICALLY APPROPRIATE PRACTICE

I am quite lucky. I have access to *real* children—about 58 of them, ages 15 months to 5 years. These children are very different from the *paper* children I deal with daily—the ones in my lectures, those I encounter in studies, discuss with my students, meet in assignments, and study in graphs, charts, and research findings. The *real* children are right in my building, in a laboratory school,[1] three floors below my office. Over the years, I have visited them, read them stories, chatted with them, written letters to them, received colourful (and very large) group responses, and invited them to tackle the three flights of stairs to visit me in my office.

One afternoon six years ago, as I was preparing to read a story to the preschool group, I witnessed an incident that got me thinking about immigrant children's language learning and planted the seeds for the book you are holding in your hands.

As the children were settling down and getting ready for story time, I noticed a little girl, whom I will call Ayten, embrace her visibly upset classmate, whom I will refer to as Li. Instead of stepping in (as adults do too often), I watched, listened, and waited. I did not hear what Ayten said to Li. She did a lot of pointing and gesticulating and spoke quietly. Her tone was gentle, calming, and sounded reassuring. It seemed to help because, by the time I was ready to read the story, Li was sitting close to Ayten, quite composed and attentive.

When our story and discussion were over, I asked the childcare staff about Ayten and Li. I discovered that almost half of the children in the lab school come from heritage language homes. I learned that Ayten and Li did not know English when they arrived in the lab school. Ayten, almost 3 years old, came from a home where Turkish was spoken and had been in the laboratory school

---

1 The Ryerson University Early Learning Centre is a licensed laboratory childcare facility.

for nine months. Li, younger than Ayten, was from a Mandarin-speaking home and joined the lab school two months earlier. Childcare staff reported that Ayten, an outgoing and cheerful child, was managing English very well. They were, however, concerned with Li's lack of interest in his new language. A shy, anxious, and withdrawn boy, Li understood little and had not yet attempted to use English. The other thing I learned was how childcare staff went about helping Li and other children adjust to English. They used key words in children's home languages to help transition them to the new environment.

This information left me with many questions about the language learning of young children who find themselves in classrooms where the language of program delivery is different from the language they hear and learn at home. I wondered about Ayten's and Li's skills in their home languages, Turkish and Mandarin. Why was Ayten's proficiency in English praised while her home language skills were unknown and ignored? Why was Li anxious and silent? What about the bilingual potential of these and other immigrant children who encounter a new language before they have managed their first language? What role do childcare staff play in immigrant children's language learning?

The Language Circumstance of Young Immigrant Children

To answer these questions, I embarked on an investigation of the language circumstance of young immigrant children. I explored the scope of their presence, the way they are perceived, their home language and literacy experiences, their language needs, the language views held by their parents, and classroom practices adopted in working with them.

My journey extended over six years and included various initiatives, interactions, and a great deal of research. I conducted a small-scale study in the laboratory school and a citywide study of Toronto childcare centres. I reviewed selected Canadian, American, and European early childhood publications. At conferences and workshops, in lecture halls and classrooms, in staff rooms, in meetings, and in seminars, I discussed immigrant children's language learning and classroom practices with early childhood practitioners (referred to as EC practitioners in this book), parents, family resource staff, speech and language pathologists, settlement workers, in-service and pre-service teachers, undergraduate and graduate students, school principals, child language researchers, and colleagues. I visited childcare centres and schools, interacted with immigrant children in regular (mainstream) classrooms and also in specialized language groups for new arrivals.

And What Did I Discover?

I confirmed what I had long suspected—immigrant children are everywhere! My two studies (Chumak-Horbatsch, 2008, 2010) revealed their strong presence in Toronto childcare centres. Nearly half are from homes where a heritage language is spoken, and, in some of these homes, families speak multiple heritage languages. Other Canadian cities with large immigrant populations report a similar presence of immigrant children. Also, reports from Europe show that the number of children from immigrant families has reached a "critical mass" (Papademetriou & Weidenfeld, 2007) while, in the United States, immigrant children are the "fastest growing segment of the nation's child population" (U.S. Census Bureau, 2000).

My investigation also revealed that the language worlds of young immigrant children are rich and varied. They do not enter the classroom as blank language slates. In fact, most arrive with some proficiency in their home languages, and some understanding of literacy. Many immigrant children have had exposure to the majority language via television, computer games, older siblings, and the wider community. Their parents want them to develop their home language and literacy skills and remain connected to family and community. They also want them to learn the majority language, to ensure success in school and in later life.

Finally, my investigation revealed that, in most cases, classroom practices do not take the bilingual potential of immigrant children into account and do not adequately address their language and literacy needs. I found that most EC practitioners focus on the quick learning of the classroom language. Attention to home languages, such as using keywords to help with transition from home to classroom, too often serves as a stepping-stone to the mastery of the classroom language.

I did, however, also encounter EC practitioners who welcomed home languages into their classrooms and worked closely with families to promote bilingualism and bi-literacy. I heard morning announcements read in the school language and in home languages. I saw excited children create bilingual word lists and share these with their monolingual classmates who looked at unfamiliar writing systems with great interest. I witnessed small groups of children chat with EC practitioners in their home language as they created dual language books.

All of this led me to ask two questions:

- What is the best way to work with young immigrant children?
- How can their language and literacy needs be met?

Running in High Park gave me the opportunity to think about my questions. And then, one cloudless morning three years ago on the banks of Grenadier Pond, as I ran past sleepy Canada geese, the idea for a new classroom practice was born. "Linguistically Appropriate Practice," I told the sleepy birds, will be inclusive, research based and practitioner friendly. It will go beyond the monolingual focus and will include practical suggestions for transforming classrooms into multilingual environments.

Why This Matters

Why is this important? Why should the language and literacy needs of immigrant children be of concern to busy EC practitioners? Why do we need a new classroom practice that attends to immigrant children's two languages?

Immigrant children are an important demographic. They will play a key role in defining the future of urban centres. If we help them grow bilingually, they will be proud of their backgrounds, develop an understanding and acceptance of differences, remain connected to their families and communities, master the classroom language, do well in school, and become important contributors to Canadian society.

> "The large number of children who enter childcare speaking a language other than English could provide an opportunity for fostering a bilingual citizenry." *(Chang, 1993, p. 67)*

Also, inclusive teaching holds benefits for *all* children. Exposure to the home languages of their classmates will help monolingual children develop an awareness of language differences, and/or spark an interest in unused family languages.

Is This Book for You?

If you work with young immigrant children, then this book is for you. If you work in a childcare centre, if you are a kindergarten teacher, or if you teach at the primary level (Grade 1 through Grade 3) and find it challenging to communicate with children who do not speak the classroom language, then read on. If you acknowledge home languages in your work, celebrate cultural differences, and still wonder about what is best for immigrant children, then this book will help you. In these pages, you will discover a new way to work with immigrant children—"Linguistically Appropriate Practice" or LAP. LAP will help you understand immigrant children and their two language worlds. LAP will explain their language learning, provide suggestions for building partnerships with families, and show you how to welcome all languages into your classroom.

Plan of the Book

This book is organized into three sequential parts:

Part I: Laying the Groundwork for LAP

The four chapters in Part I provide important background information about immigrant children and will address the following questions:

- Where are immigrant children?
- Who are immigrant children?
- What characterizes their language circumstance?
- How do we currently work with them?
- What is "Linguistically Appropriate Practice"?
- Why do we need a new way to work with young immigrant children?

Chapter 1: Immigrant Children in the Classroom

The first chapter reports on the global presence of immigrant children. Documents from Canada, the United States, and Europe tell us that immigrant children fill the classrooms of urban centres. The findings of a large-scale study that documented children's home languages and staff language backgrounds are used to illustrate the very real presence of immigrant children in metropolitan centres with large immigrant populations.

Chapter 2: A Language Portrait of Young Immigrant Children

Understanding the language circumstance of young immigrant children is an important first step in the adoption of LAP. The "language portrait" introduced in this chapter sketches the two sides of immigrant children's language lives. One side portrays their language skills, strengths, capabilities, needs, and potential. The other side shows the challenges they face in monolingual classrooms.

Chapter 3: Classroom Practices with Young Immigrant Children

This chapter looks at two perspectives of classroom practices as they relate to young immigrant children. Selected Canadian, American, and European publications that address practices with linguistically diverse children are reviewed. Reports of classroom practices from EC practitioners are also discussed. A summary of classroom practices is presented, areas of concern are identified, and a new way of working with immigrant children is proposed.

Chapter 4: Linguistically Appropriate Practice—Background
Chapter 4 defines LAP and explains why we need a new approach in our work with immigrant children. Dynamic bilingualism, the theoretical framing of LAP, is explained.

Part II: Setting the Stage for LAP
The two chapters in Part II focus on LAP preparations. They address two questions:

- How do I prepare my classroom for LAP?
- What has to be in place to launch LAP?

Chapter 5: Preparing the Classroom for LAP
In this chapter, the EC practitioner is invited to make a commitment to inclusive and multilingual teaching. Suggestions for preparing the classroom for LAP include developing a classroom language policy with the children, charting the home languages represented in the classroom, setting up a new classroom space called the "language centre," and transforming the classroom into a multilingual and a multi-literate zone.

Chapter 6: Adopting LAP in the Classroom
This chapter looks closely at four tasks that are central to the adoption of LAP: transitioning immigrant children from home to classroom, partnering with families, using home languages in the classroom, and recording classroom language and literacy behaviours.

Part III: Implementing LAP Activities

Chapter 7: LAP Activities
In this chapter, the EC practitioner will find a series of exciting classroom activities. These activities can be adopted as is, or they can be adapted to match the developmental level and the interests of the children.

Looking Ahead
The closing section looks to the future. It appeals to those working with young immigrant children to take the time to understand the language circumstance of these children, pay attention to their unique language and literacy needs, and help them realize their bilingual potential.

How to Use This Book

Before you jump in and adopt the activities found in Part III, I urge you to do three things: (1) take the time to review the terms defined below, (2) carefully read Part I and Part II, and (3) with your colleagues, complete the group activities at the end of each chapter. These three steps will provide you with important background information, help you see immigrant children in a new way, and prepare you for the adoption of LAP.

Throughout this book, you will find photos anecdotes, and stories provided by EC practitioners who are implementing LAP in their classrooms. This material serves to illustrate that LAP can bring about positive results for *all* children. As well, key points are included at the end of each chapter. For the reader who wants additional information, references are provided. Appendices found at the end of each chapter can also be downloaded from http://www.ryerson.ca/mylanguage.

Definitions

The following terms are central to understanding and implementing LAP.

Childcare staff[1] are employees of childcare centres.

Classroom is used to refer to three contexts: the childcare centre, the kindergarten room, and the primary classroom (Grade 1 through Grade 3).

Classroom language refers to the language of program delivery.

Classroom practices refer to plans, activities, and strategies that EC practitioners adopt in their work with immigrant children. These practices are considered to be effective for guiding children who come from homes where heritage languages are spoken and who arrive with limited proficiency in the classroom language.

Early childhood (EC) practitioners include those professionals who work directly with young children and are responsible for all aspects of program planning and delivery, namely, childcare staff as well as kindergarten and primary grade teachers.

Families are persons of importance in the lives of young children: parents, grandparents, siblings, guardians, and relatives.

---

1 Staff is used as a singular collective noun to refer to the employees of a single childcare centre, and as a plural collective noun when referring to employees of more than one childcare centre (*Canadian Oxford Dictionary*, 2004).

Heritage language refers to any language other than English or French (the two official languages of Canada) and Canadian Aboriginal languages.

Immigrant children are

- between birth and 8 years old;
- mostly born in the host country to newly arrived parents;
- in some cases, born outside of the host country;
- raised in homes where heritage languages are spoken;
- initially exposed to the societal language in the home and in the community (siblings, media, wider community);
- in various stages of acquiring their home language; and
- in various stages of acquiring the classroom language.

Language circumstance refers to a linguistic situation, which includes exposure to language or languages and literacy-related experiences in three contexts: the home, community, and classroom.

Language parenting refers to language and literacy practices and behaviours adopted by parents in the home.

Monolingual means having or using one language.

Monolingual children are speakers of the classroom language. Some *monolingual* children are native speakers of the classroom language, having acquired it as their first and only language. Other *monolingual children* are fluent in the classroom language and have passive knowledge or limited proficiency in one (or more) Heritage or Aboriginal language(s).

Societal language is the official language of a country or a state. In Canada, there are two societal or official languages: English and French.

Transition refers to immigrant children's journey from home to the classroom. It is far more than a short-term, new language-learning event for the child who has no friends and does not speak the classroom language. It is an ongoing circumstance that directly affects the young child's personal, social, emotional, linguistic, and cognitive development.

Younger children are infants (birth to 18 months) and toddlers (18 to 30 months). *Older children* are preschoolers (2½ to 4 years), kindergarteners (4 and 5 years olds), and primary graders (6 to 8 years old).

PART I

Laying the Groundwork for LAP

CHAPTER I

IMMIGRANT CHILDREN IN THE CLASSROOM

Immigrant Children Are Everywhere

The number of immigrant children in urban neighbourhoods, playgrounds, and classrooms is on the rise. Population estimates show that their numbers will continue to increase. In response to this increase, the National Association for the Education of Young Children (NAEYC, 2009) issued the following statement: "The biggest single child-specific demographic change in the United States over the next twenty years is predicted to be an increase in children whose home language is not English" (p. 2).

> "Young children learning L2[1] are one of the fastest growing segments of the global population." *(Kan & Kohnert, 2005, p. 380)*

In Canada, immigrant children are the "fastest growing segment of the nation's population" (Statistics Canada, 2006a).

In European countries, they "constitute a significant presence" (Collicelli, 2001) and have been referred to as a "critical mass" (Papademetriou & Weidenfeld, 2007). Although most immigrant families have traditionally settled in "gateway cities" or large urban centres, newcomers are now settling in smaller communities that provide settlement support and promise better economic opportunities. For example, in 2007, the number of immigrants who settled in Charlottetown, Prince Edward Island, was up by 73 per cent from the previous year. Moncton, New Brunswick, saw its immigrant population increase by 31 per cent; Saskatoon, Saskatchewan, saw a rise of 40 per cent; and Red Deer, Alberta, welcomed 93 per cent more newcomers than the previous year (*Canada Immigration Newsletter*, 2008).

....

1 L2 is a second language.

An Example from Toronto

To illustrate the very real presence of immigrant children in urban areas, we go to a recent study, referred to here as the Childcare Study (Chumak-Horbatsch, 2010), which documented the home languages of children and the language backgrounds of the staff of Toronto childcare centres.

> Q: What did the Childcare Study reveal?
>
> A: The Childcare Study revealed three things:
>
> 1. Immigrant children make up approximately half of the childcare population of Toronto.
> 2. Childcare staff are mostly speakers of heritage languages.
> 3. There is a significant match between immigrant children's home languages and the heritage languages known and used by childcare staff.

Let's have a closer look at these findings.

Toronto: A City of Immigrants

With a population of over two million inhabitants, Toronto is one of the world's most culturally and linguistically diverse cities. The motto "Diversity Our Strength" describes Toronto's attention to and celebration of newcomers who come to the Canadian city to live, work, and raise families. Toronto has been described as a "language mosaic," where over 140 languages and dialects can be heard. In 2006, over 30 per cent of Torontonians spoke a language other than English or French at home (Statistics Canada, 2006b). In 2004, the United Nations Development Programme ranked Toronto second, behind Miami, in its "List of World Cities with the Largest Percentage of Foreign-Born Population." Even though Miami has a higher foreign-born population (mostly Hispanic and Haitian), Toronto's foreign-born population is significantly more diverse. More information about diversity in Toronto can be found on the City of Toronto (2012) website (see http://www.toronto.ca/toronto_facts/diversity.htm).

Children's Home Languages

A questionnaire was sent electronically to the supervisors of 800 Toronto childcare centres (licensed by the Ontario Ministry of Children and Youth Services) that provide childcare services for some combination of the following four age groups: infants (birth to 18 months), toddlers (18 to 30 months), preschoolers (2½ to 4 years), and kindergarteners (4 and 5 years). Supervisors were asked to copy the questionnaire and send it home with every child. The questionnaire was in English and asked parents to select one of 14 home language options (see Appendix 1.A). The questionnaire was biased toward those parents who are speakers of English, who have a working knowledge of English, and who understand how to complete a questionnaire. These parents were more likely to take the time to complete the questionnaire and return it to their child's childcare centre.

Of the 800 childcare centres contacted, 190 (24 per cent) returned completed questionnaires. This number represents a total of 4,110 children. The response rate varied from centre to centre—from a single returned questionnaire in one centre to 96 returned in another. Although the home language use of non-participating children remains unknown, the response rate was sufficient to provide a representative sample of language use in the childcare population of Toronto.

Figure 1.1 shows that English was reported most often as the home language of children attending Toronto childcare centres (48 per cent), with heritage language speakers following close behind (43 per cent). The total for French was 7 per cent, and the final category, "Other," which included Aboriginal languages and American Sign Language, totalled 2 per cent.

FIGURE 1.1: Children's Home Languages, Toronto Childcare Study, 2010

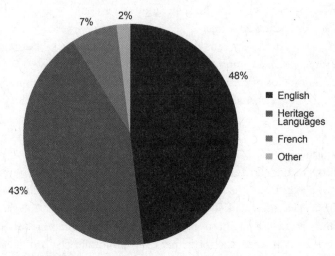

N = 4110

Source: Chumak-Horbatsch (2010).

Heritage languages were reported in all but four of the 190 childcare centres. Of the 129 different heritage languages reported, Chinese and Spanish were reported most often. Between 1 and 10 heritage languages were present in most of the centres (88 per cent), and the remaining centres reported an even higher number of heritage languages (between 11 and 22).

TABLE 1.1: Most Frequently Reported Heritage Languages

CHILDCARE STUDY	CANADA CENSUS 2006: LANGUAGE DATA			
TORONTO	TORONTO	EDMONTON	VANCOUVER	MONTREAL
Chinese	Chinese	Chinese	Chinese	Italian
Spanish	Italian	German	Punjabi	Arabic
Tamil	Portuguese	Tagalog	Tagalog	Spanish
Portuguese	Tagalog	Ukrainian	German	Creoles
Arabic	Spanish	Arabic	Hindi	Greek

Source: Statistics Canada (2006b) and Chumak-Harbatsch (2010).

The home languages reported in the Childcare Study parallel those documented for other Canadian census metropolitan areas (CMAs).[1] Comparing results from the Childcare Study to non-official language data from the 2006 Canada Census (Statistics Canada, 2006b) reveals this similar pattern of home language use in Canada's large cities. Table 1.1 shows the five most frequently reported heritage languages in the Childcare Study and in four CMAs: Toronto, Edmonton, Vancouver, and Montreal.

Table 1.1 shows that Chinese is the most frequently reported heritage language in three CMAs (Toronto, Edmonton, and Vancouver), as well as in the Childcare Study. Not surprisingly, the closest match (Chinese, Spanish, and Portuguese) is between heritage languages reported in the Childcare Study and in Toronto.

Staff Languages

The supervisors of the 800 Toronto childcare centres were asked to submit (electronically) a Staff Language List, a record of the languages (in addition to English) known and used by staff. The Staff Language Lists included a language count only, and not the number of speakers for each of the languages reported. Of the 800 centres contacted, 225 (or 28 per cent) submitted Staff Language Lists. A total of 63 different staff heritage languages were reported. As shown

1 A census metropolitan area is defined as a very large urban area (known as the urban core) together with adjacent urban and rural areas that have a high degree of social and economic integration with the urban core. A CMA has an urban core population of at least 100,000.

in Figure 1.2, most childcare staff were heritage language speakers. A small number were speakers of French, English only, and American Sign Language (ASL).

FIGURE 1.2: Staff Languages, Toronto Childcare Study, 2010

STAFF LANGUAGES

ASL = American Sign Language

Source: Chumak-Horbatsch (2010).

TABLE 1.2: Ten Most Frequently Reported Heritage Languages: Children and Staff, 2010

	CHILDREN'S HERITAGE LANGUAGES		STAFF HERITAGE LANGUAGES
1.	**Chinese**	1.	**Chinese**
2.	**Spanish**	2.	**Spanish**
3.	**Tamil**	3.	**Italian**
4.	**Portuguese**	4.	**Portuguese**
5.	**Arabic**	5.	*Greek*
6.	**Italian**	6.	*Urdu*
7.	*Russian*	7.	**Hindi**
8.	*Tagalog*	8.	**Tamil**
9.	**Hindi**	9.	*Polish*
10.	*Farsi*	10.	**Arabic**

Source: Chumak-Horbatsch (2010).

Child-Staff Language Match or Mismatch?

Language match is defined as a situation where childcare staff and children share the same heritage language or languages. An example of a language match would be a Mandarin-speaking staff member working in a centre with children for whom Mandarin is their home language. Language mismatch is the oppo-site—where staff and children are speakers of different heritage languages. A Portuguese-speaking child, for example, with an Urdu-speaking staff member would be in a language mismatch situation.

Table 1.2 shows that, across Toronto childcare centres, there was a significant match between the heritage languages spoken by children and staff. Seven of the 10 languages (shown in **bold**) in each list are the same. Chinese and Spanish are the two most frequently reported heritage languages for both children and staff, while Portuguese is listed in fourth place in both lists. Tamil, Arabic, Italian, and Hindi appear in both lists, though not in the same order.

Child-staff language mismatches (shown in *italics*) are noted for three languages. Children's heritage languages not spoken by staff include Russian, Tagalog, and Farsi. Heritage languages known and used by staff but not by children include Greek, Urdu, and Polish.

Summary

This chapter shows that immigrant children are a significant demographic in Canadian, American, and European cities, both large and small. The Childcare Study provides us with an example of the presence of immigrant children in one large urban centre, Toronto. The comparison of results from this study with data on non-official languages, as reported in the Canada Census (Statistics Canada, 2006b), shows us that other Canadian cities also have large immigrant populations. We also saw that childcare staff in Toronto are speakers of heritage languages, which, in most cases, match children's home languages.

These results tell us, then, that immigrant children warrant our attention. As these children fill classrooms, EC practitioners must take the time to get to know them and understand their needs. Only then will they be able to work effectively with them. The next chapter sketches a language portrait of immigrant children, a narrative of their unique language circumstance.

Key Points

1. Immigrant children are a fast growing demographic in both large and small urban centres in Canada, the United States, and Europe.
2. The Childcare Study revealed three things about the childcare population of Toronto:
   (a) Close to half of the children are from homes where a heritage language is spoken.
   (b) Staff are mostly speakers of heritage languages.
   (c) Children's home languages and staff languages are closely matched.
3. These findings can be extended to other Canadian cities and also, to some extent, to American and European urban centres with large immigrant populations.

Group Activities

1. Classroom Language Map
(a) Copy the questionnaire on home language use (see Appendix 1.A) and send it home with each child.
(b) When the questionnaires are returned, create a chart (see Appendix 1.B) showing children's home languages and the names and number of speakers for each language. Which home languages are listed most often?

2. Staff Language List

(a) List all the languages that staff know and use.

(b) Create a chart (see Appendix 1.C) showing the languages staff know and use. Which languages are listed most often?

3. Child-Staff Language Match or Mismatch

(a) Prepare a table (see Appendix 1.D) listing the most frequent child and staff languages. Where do you see a match or mismatch between the home languages of the children and the languages staff know and use?

(b) Discuss ways to strengthen the child-staff language match in your classroom.

APPENDIX I.A

....

Questionnaire: Home Language Use

....

1. Child's name _____

2. Child's age in years and months: _____ years _____ months

3. Please check (✔) the box that matches the language most often spoken in your home with family members.

    ☐ English ONLY

    ☐ French ONLY

    ☐ English AND French

    ☐ Aboriginal language (First Nations, Métis, Inuit) ONLY

    ☐ Aboriginal language (First Nations, Métis, Inuit) AND English

    ☐ Aboriginal language (First Nations, Métis, Inuit) AND French

    ☐ Aboriginal language (First Nations, Métis, Inuit) and OTHER

    Name of OTHER languages used in your home in addition to

    Aboriginal language _____

    ☐ Heritage languages ONLY: A heritage language is a language other than English and French, such as Urdu or Mandarin.

    Name of heritage languages used in the home _____

    _____

☐ Heritage language AND English

Name of heritage language used in addition to English _____

_____

☐ Heritage language AND French

Name of heritage language used in addition to French

_____

☐ Heritage language and OTHER

Name of heritage language _____

Name of other language used in addition to the heritage language

_____

☐ Sign language ONLY

☐ Sign language and OTHER

Name of languages used in addition to sign language

_____

☐ OTHER home language use: _____

APPENDIX I.B

....

Home Languages: Children

....

HOME LANGUAGE	CHILD'S NAME	TOTAL #

APPENDIX I.C

Languages Known and Used by Staff

HOME LANGUAGE	STAFF NAME	TOTAL #

APPENDIX I.D

Children and Staff—Most Frequently Reported Languages

CHILDREN'S HOME LANGUAGES	LANGUAGES KNOWN AND USED BY STAFF
1.	1.
2.	2.
3.	3.
4.	4.
5.	5.
6.	6.
7.	7.
8.	8.
9.	9.
10.	10.

A LANGUAGE PORTRAIT OF YOUNG IMMIGRANT CHILDREN

In this chapter, we will paint a language portrait of immigrant children. Unlike the artist who uses colours and brushstrokes to cover the canvas, we will use words to create a verbal image of immigrant children's language lives—their linguistic experiences, skills, strengths, capabilities, and challenges. How will we do this? Why is it important for EC practitioners to be familiar with the language lives of immigrant children? What can a language portrait reveal about immigrant children? Can knowledge of their language lives affect classroom practice? If so, how? For answers to these questions, read on.

....

What Is a Language Portrait?

....

The language portrait is a pedagogical tool. Adapted from qualitative research methodology (Lawrence-Lightfoot & Hoffman Davis, 1997), it provides EC practitioners with an accurate, research-based picture of immigrant children's linguistic reality and bilingual potential. Guided by the question "What is good here?" the language portrait focuses on the richness of immigrant children's language lives and their language and literacy learning. Yet, to be an authentic narrative, the portrait must also include those aspects of immigrant children's language lives that are troubling and challenging.

Information for the language portrait comes from two sources. My personal and professional experience contributed considerably in shaping the language portrait: a Ukrainian-language childhood in English-speaking Toronto, raising two children with three languages, and working as a classroom teacher and a child language researcher. The second source—numerous documents (reports, policy papers, and research studies) from Canada, the United States, and Europe that considered various aspects of immigrant children's language circumstance—provides the portrait with a theoretical grounding. References are provided for the interested reader.

An Eight-Part Language Portrait

The language portrait covers eight aspects of immigrant children's language circumstance (see text box). It includes information about their home language and literacy experiences, their dual language learning, and the linguistic, personal, and social challenges they face in the monolingual classroom. Each aspect is described in the following pages.

EIGHT ASPECTS OF IMMIGRANT CHILDREN'S LANGUAGE LIVES

IMMIGRANT CHILDREN

are emergent bilinguals,

have language lives beyond the classroom,

can successfully navigate two languages,

have dual language and literacy needs,

risk losing their home languages,

experience isolation and loneliness,

experience language shock and remain silent, and

often hide their home language.

Immigrant Children Are Emergent Bilinguals

In Canada, the United States, the United Kingdom, and Australia, researchers, policy makers, practitioners, service providers, and educators identify and label immigrant children as non-speakers or incomplete speakers of the majority language. For example, of the 24 terms used to refer to immigrant children (see Table 2.1), 19 identify them in terms of their learning of English.

"Calling these children emergent bilinguals makes reference to a positive characteristic—not one of being limited or being learners ..." (García, 2009b, p. 322)

TABLE 2.1: Terms Used to Refer to Immigrant Children in a Majority English Context

ABBREVIATION	TERM
CSESL	Children who Speak English as a Second Language
CLD	Culturally and Linguistically Diverse
DLL	Dual Language Learners
EAL	English as an Additional Language
EF	English First
EFL	English as a Foreign Language
EL	English Learners
ELD	English Language Development
ELCB	English Language Communication Barriers
ELL	English Language Learners
ESL	English as a Second Language
EO	English Only
ESOL	English for Speakers of Other Languages
LOTE	Language Other Than English
LEP	Limited English Proficiency
LESA	Limited English Speaking Ability
LM	Language Minority
NAC	Newly Arrived Children
NES	Non-English Speakers
NESB	Non-English Speaking Backgrounds
NESC	Non-English Speaking Children
NYE	Not Yet English
OTE	Other Than English
SLL	Second Language Learner

Yet immigrant children are far more than learners of the classroom language. They are *emergent bilinguals*. They arrive in the classroom with some proficiency in their home language and some familiarity with literacy. To these home language skills and experiences, they add the classroom language—and begin their bilingual journey. By viewing them as emergent bilinguals whose two languages are evolving, we recognize the importance of their home language and literacy accomplishments, set aside the many single-language labels that hamper their progress, and concentrate on their bilingual potential. For more information on emergent bilinguals, see García (2009b).

Focusing on the lack of English or on the learning or superiority of the classroom language is limiting and problematic for three reasons (García & Kleifgen, 2010; Nemeth, 2009):

- It establishes the classroom language as the only language worth knowing, learning, and speaking.
- It solidifies classroom language teaching as the goal of working with immigrant children.
- It devalues immigrant children's home languages and literacy experiences, skills, and strengths.

Immigrant Children Have Language Lives beyond the Classroom

Studies of immigrant families confirm this statement (see text box below) from the Ontario Ministry of Education and show that most immigrant children live in homes where materials written in the home language, such as calendars, newspapers, magazines, and books, are plentiful. Many learn to read religious texts and recite prayers in their home (or additional) languages. This familiarity with written words means that they arrive in the classroom as *active* language learners and users. They know

"Before going to school, children have already had a wide range of lived experiences with spoken, written, and visual communication, and have used language in familiar contexts." *(Ontario Ministry of Education, 2006, p. 33)*

songs and share books in the home language with parents and siblings. They watch movies and television programs in the home language. They are encouraged to write letters to grandparents and relatives living in the countries where their families originated.

THE HOME LANGUAGE LIVES OF IMMIGRANT CHILDREN

IN MOST CASES, IMMIGRANT CHILDREN HAVE

- numerous language partners: older siblings, grandparents, relatives, friends;
- contact with the family's country of origin: visits, letter writing, telephone or Internet calls;
- participation in language communities: celebrations, clubs, events;
- books, newspapers, magazines, calendars, brochures;
- home language media (radio, TV, DVDs, computer);
- music from the country of origin, often including singing in the home language, playing traditional instruments, dancing; and
- religious practices: e.g., reading and reciting texts or prayers.

Yet the home language lives of immigrant children are not strictly monolingual. In addition to the home language and literacy experiences listed on the previous page, the majority language is, to some extent, also present in the homes of these children. They witness parents and older siblings learning and using the new language, and most have access to majority language media (television, computers, cell phones, games). The products (food, clothing, household items, and toys) in their homes have labels in the societal language, as do the brochures dropped into their mailboxes. For further information on the language lives of immigrant children, see Chumak-Horbatsch (2006, 2008); Moll, Amanti, Neff, and González (1992); Lucas and Villegas (2010); Goodwin (2002); and Wong Fillmore (2000).

Immigrant Children Can Successfully Navigate Two Languages

From the extensive literature on childhood bilingualism, we have selected and summarized seven principles that are central to understanding this phenomenon. Each principle is described briefly. Interested readers will find additional information in the references provided at the end of each principle.

SEVEN PRINCIPLES OF CHILDHOOD BILINGUALISM

1. Second language learning is not a simple soaking-up process.
2. Young children learn their second language in many different ways.
3. Learning the new language involves acquiring skills on two levels: social and academic.
4. The two languages of a bilingual work together.
5. The home language affects children's personal, social, linguistic, and cognitive development.
6. There are cognitive and language processing advantages to bilingualism.
7. Language mixing is common and natural in bilinguals.

Principle 1: Second Language Learning Is Not a Simple Soaking-Up Process

Like all typically developing children, immigrant children *can* learn two languages as naturally as one and *can* successfully navigate two language worlds. Yet dual language learning is not a simple, automatic, soaking-up process. To become bilingual, children

"One of the most harmful and pervasive myths about second language acquisition in children is that they learn a second language easily, quickly, and automatically." *(Snow, 1997, p. ix–xi)*

require two meaningful, supportive, loving, and stimulating environments, with significant exposure in each language. (See Genesee, 2008; Kan & Kohnert, 2005; Kuhl, 2004; Paradis, Genesee, & Crago, 2010; Tabors, 2008.)

Principle 2: Young Children Learn Their Second Language in Many Different Ways

There is great variation in the way young children learn a new language. Some eagerly initiate interactions with speakers of the classroom language and appear to pick up a new language quickly. Others are more cautious and reluctant in their new language environment. Both internal and external factors help explain the progress a child makes in a second language. Internal or individual factors include the child's age, personality, aptitude, motivation, and learning style. External or environmental factors include exposure to the new language, the willingness of classroom language-speaking peers to interact, adult (parent and teacher) attitudes to the new language, language background (similarity of the home language to the new language), and family socio-economic status. (See Baker, 2006; Bialystok, 2001a, 2001b; Thompson, 2000; Wong Fillmore, 1991, 2000.)

Principle 3: Learning the New Language Involves Acquiring Skills on Two Levels: Social and Academic

Learning a new language is more than learning to talk. It involves acquiring skills on two levels: social and academic. Social language or everyday face-to-face communication is mastered within about two years of initial exposure. As they chat informally with peers and adults, immigrant children derive meaning not only from the words they hear but also from the context, facial expressions, body language, and gestures. The content of social language is frequently focused on personal experiences, making it easier for immigrant children to be engaged actively.

On the other hand, academic language, also known as school language, is impersonal, more technical and abstract, and takes approximately five to seven years to master. Mastery of academic language, which is essential for immigrant children's success in school, includes listening, speaking, reading, and writing about subject content. This level of language learning is removed from personal experiences and is more complex and cognitively more demanding than social language. Academic language requires the immigrant child to deal with classroom tasks, activities, and routines that make use of specialized (content-specific) vocabulary and language forms not found in social language. (See Cummins, 1979, 1981, 2000.)

Principle 4: The Two Languages of a Bilingual Work Together

The two languages of a bilingual child work together, and there is a strong connection between them. While they may appear different on the surface, the two languages are not separate. They operate through the same central processing or cognitive areas of the brain. In the right conditions and with adequate age-appropriate exposure, a child's two languages interact and strengthen each other. This means that certain kinds of language and literacy skills are transferred across languages, even when the two languages are quite different and the child's home language is not fully developed. For example, immigrant children proficient in their home languages apply their knowledge and understanding of word meanings to the new language they encounter (see text box). The same kind of transfer occurs with basic literacy skills such as understanding that words tell a story and that letters spell words. Such cross-language transfer is not automatic and requires adequate exposure in each language. Also, this kind of transfer across languages explains why instruction in the home language does not negatively affect classroom language learning. (See Colomé, 2001; Cummins, 1979, 1981, 2000; 2001b; Genesee, 2008; Krashen, 2004; Kroll, Bobb, Misra, & Guo, 2008; Riches & Genesee, 2006.)

FROM ENGLISH TO POLISH

At bedtime, four-year-old Zosia, a speaker of Polish, informs her mother that winter is coming fast. "How do you know that?" asks her surprised mother. "Because I heard it in school and made the words Polish," answers the child.

Principle 5: The Home Language Affects Children's Personal, Social, Linguistic, and Cognitive Development

The fifth principle underlines the importance of children's home languages for their personal, social, linguistic, and cognitive development. For example, it is through the home language that

"... there is increasingly a recognition that for pupils to succeed, the home language should be acknowledged and built upon." *(Mahon, Crutchley, & Quinn, 2003, p. 237)*

cultural values are transmitted to children. Also, being able to communicate in the home language allows children to have a close relationship with grandparents and extended family members. Numerous studies have consistently shown that the child who is strong in the home language will eventually be strong in the classroom language. According to Cummins (2001a), the home language builds up a linguistic foundation and sets the child up for success.

(See Baker, 2006; Cummins, 2001a, 2001b; *Hold on to Your Home Language*, 2012 [http://www.ryerson.ca/mylanguage/]; Riches & Genesee, 2006; Wong Fillmore, 1991, 2000.)

Principle 6: There Are Cognitive and Language Processing Advantages to Bilingualism

Research studies over the past 30 years have clearly demonstrated that children who are learning two languages show a definite advantage in a number of cognitive and language-processing skills compared to children who are learning only one language. (See the text box "Cognitive and Linguistic Advantages of Bilingualism.") This advantage has been reported in children as young as 24 months. Bilingual children are flexible thinkers, have good working memories for storing and processing information, and are better able to deal with distractions than monolingual children. (See Baker, 2006; Bialystok, 1991, 1992, 2001a, 2001b; Bialystok & Martin, 2004; Bialystok & Shapero, 2005; Kovács & Mehler, 2009; Poulin-Dubois, Blaye, Coutya, & Bialystok, 2011.)

COGNITIVE AND LINGUISTIC ADVANTAGES OF BILINGUALISM

Children who are learning two languages show an advantage in the following skills:

- classification;
- concept formation;
- problem solving;
- analogical reasoning;
- visual-spatial understanding;
- creativity and mental flexibility;
- sensitivity to the details and structure of language;
- recognition of ambiguities;
- identification and correction of ungrammatical sentences;
- storytelling;
- word learning;
- flexibility in dealing with symbols and words;
- early reading; and
- executive-function system, i.e., the ability to control attention, to inhibit distraction, to manage sets of stimuli, to expand working memory, and to shift between tasks.

Principle 7: Language Mixing Is Common and Natural in Bilinguals

Using two languages in a single utterance and switching from one language to another are both common and natural among bilinguals. Such language jumbling or mixing has been referred to as code mixing, code switching, or borrowing. More recently, the language mixing of bilinguals has been described as the natural movement between languages and has been called "translanguaging" (see Chapter 4).

THE MAIN FEATURES OF LANGUAGE MIXING

LANGUAGE MIXING

- is normal for bilinguals,
- distinguishes bilingual children from their monolingual peers,
- shows the presence and management of two language systems,
- is not a sign of language confusion,
- should not be viewed in negative terms,
- does not mean that the child has difficulty differentiating two language systems,
- does not happen randomly: it is rule governed, and
- is a social behaviour, reflective of relationships.

Taken together, the seven principles of childhood bilingualism remind us that immigrant children's two-language learning is far from automatic and simple. It is a complex, lengthy, and rewarding process. Progress and proficiency in the classroom language are determined by both personal and environmental factors. Immigrant children's two languages are not separate entities. Skills mastered in one language are often transferred to the new language. As they learn the new language, immigrant children are faced with a two-level task—chatting with their friends and dealing with the more abstract classroom language. Mixing languages is common among immigrant children—to get their message understood, they often borrow across their two languages. (See Baker, 2006; García, 2009a, 2009b, 2009c; Paradis, Genesee, & Crago, 2010.)

Immigrant Children Have Dual Language and Literacy Needs

Immigrant children require an environment that will enable them to realize their bilingual potential. Yet their language and literacy needs are too often equated with the learning of the classroom language. Clearly, these children need to master the classroom language in order to live, study, and work in a society that speaks a language that is different from their home language.

However, learning the majority language is only *one* of their language needs. In addition to their emergent classroom language, immigrant children live and grow in another language, one that forms their identity and connects them to family, culture, country of origin, and religion. Therefore, they have *dual* language and literacy needs and require concrete support and guidance in learning both the home language *and* the classroom language. (See Au, 2006; Baker, 2006, García, 2009a, 2009b, 2009c; Garret & Holcomb, 2005; Goodwin, 2002; Matthews, 2008; Matthews & Ewen, 2010; Nemeth, 2009; Schoorman, 2001; Tabors, 2008.)

> "We should not be in the business of making children forget what they know ... Rather than thinking in terms of an 'English-only' culture, we should be promoting 'English plus.'" *(National Centre for Languages, 2006, p. 2–3)*

Immigrant Children Risk Losing Their Home Languages

Immigrant children who attend programs delivered in the societal language risk losing their home languages. Daily exposure to the classroom language and reduced exposure to the home language result in language competition, where development of the home language too often becomes "arrested." Within a short period of time, the new language replaces the home language.

> "For young typically developing second language learners, skills in the first language are vulnerable either to backsliding or to incomplete acquisition ..." *(Kohnert, Yim, Nett, Kan, & Duran, 2005, p. 253)*

Wong Fillmore (1991) describes such language loss as "far-reaching" because it signals the end of bilingualism, creates monolingual speakers, negatively affects family relations, damages the spiritual bond between parents and children, and alienates children from their families. She urges EC practitioners to help parents understand the consequences of language loss and the importance of nurturing the home language by providing rich home language experiences for their young children. (See Chumak-Horbatsch, 2008; Li & Zhu, 2006; Schiff-Meyers, 1992; Wong Fillmore, 1991, 2000; Woods, Boyle, & Hubbard, 1999.)

Immigrant Children Experience Isolation and Loneliness

Over the years, during visits to classrooms and childcare centres, I noticed silent, uneasy, and nervous behaviours in newly arrived children. I witnessed averted eyes, fingernail and lip biting, and heads lowered to one side in a withdrawal-like gesture. These behaviours were noted when the children were physically separated from their peers as well as when they appeared to be part of the group. In response to my questions, EC practitioners explained that these behaviours are part of immigrant children's "transition" to the classroom.

According to studies that have investigated the adjustment of newly arrived children, however, this is more than transitional behaviour. These anxious and nervous behaviours signal social isolation and loneliness. Anyone observing these children sees clearly that they have not yet managed to gain acceptance by their peers due to their inability to communicate in the classroom language. This lack of acceptance causes uncertainty and loneliness. Their peers mostly ignore them and, in some cases, attempt to communicate with them by simplifying their speech, as if they were speaking with an infant, for example using a high-pitched voice and reduced forms. (See Garret & Holcomb, 2005; Goodwin, 2002; Igoa, 1995; Kirova, 2001, 2003; Olsen, 2000; Tabors, 2008; Thompson, 2000; Wong Fillmore, 2000.)

Immigrant Children Experience Language Shock and Remain Silent

The silence of young immigrant children is currently accepted as part of their classroom language learning. They adopt the "mechanism of silence" (Igoa, 1995, p. 38), the thinking goes, and remain non-verbal or mute for weeks, months, or even years, because they come to understand that their way of speaking is not acceptable in the classroom.

The silent period (also referred to as the preproduction, receptive, or adjustment stage) is viewed as an important part of immigrant children's classroom language learning. Driven by "comprehension precedes production" thinking, numerous studies and guidebooks describe this period as the time for children to give up all they know, silently crack the code of the new language, and privately practice, repeat, and experiment with the classroom language. In order to communicate in their new environment, they must abandon all use of the home language, face loneliness and social isolation, and resort to vocalizations, gestures, body language, and facial expressions. After weeks or months of silence and non-verbal communication, they will begin to use single words in the classroom language and enter the "production" stage.

The origins of the "silent period" concept can be traced back to Krashen and Terrell (1983), who described a "preproduction" stage of second language learning, and to the handful of case studies that followed. These studies documented the non-verbal periods of children (preschool to age 13) learning a second language, periods that lasted from 2 to 18 months. Based on these dated examples, researchers have come to accept the silent period as a consistent feature of immigrant children's second language learning. (See Igoa, 1995; Krashen & Terrell, 1983; Tabors, 2008.)

Silent or Silenced?

Young immigrant children arrive in the classroom as language users at various stages of proficiency in their home language and with some understanding and experience of literacy. We therefore challenge the concept that the silent period is an acceptable part of their language learning. Accepting it as such is unfair and damaging to young immigrant children, who pay a heavy emotional and social toll when EC practitioners wait for this so-called stage of language learning to pass.

In reality, it is the monolingual classroom that silences immigrant children. When they arrive in the classroom, they experience "language shock" (Olsen, 2000) and "extreme linguistic uncertainty" (García, 2009a). They quickly come to realize that the language they know does not matter and that their way of speaking is discouraged (and sometimes forbidden). They also understand that they are relegated to the role of novice language learners and must revert to primitive forms of communication. (See Erwin-Tripp, 1974; García 2009a; Hakuta, 1978; Igoa, 1995; Itoh & Hatch, 1978; Olsen, 2000; Saville-Troike, 1988; Tabors, 1982; Tabors & Snow, 1994.)

Immigrant Children Often Hide Their Home Language

Young immigrant children quickly understand that their home language does not "work" in the classroom. After this realization, they make attempts to "hide" the way they speak at home. The following accounts show how two preschoolers and a kindergartener "hid" their home languages in the classroom. Included also are the EC practitioners' responses—assuring the children that they can use the home language freely in the classroom.

> In the Preschool Room, a girl leans over and secretively whispers to a boy at the sand table. I walk over and ask them if they would like to share their "secret" with me. The girl says there is no secret and that they are speaking in Turkish. I tell them that whispering is not necessary—they can speak together in Turkish in the classroom openly.

> A Mandarin-speaking girl in the kindergarten classroom draws Chinese characters on a sheet of paper and proceeds to cut these out into small cards. She then walks to the housekeeping centre, moves the play oven away from the wall, tapes her Chinese cards on the wall, and returns the oven to its place, covering the cards. When the EC practitioner asks her why she did this, the child shrugs her shoulders and replies, "I don't know." Curious, the EC practitioner asks the child for an explanation the next day. This time the child explains, "It's only for the Chinese people." Following this incident, the EC practitioner invites the child's mother to come to the classroom and tell the children about the Chinese language. It's exciting for the children to have their names printed in Chinese characters.

Summary

By carefully studying the language portrait sketched in this chapter, EC practitioners will come to understand the two sides of immigrant children's language lives. One side portrays their language strengths, abilities, skills, needs, and potential. They arrive in the classroom not as novices with blank language slates but as language users with language and literacy experiences, eager to learn the new language and join the classroom community. The other side of their language lives shows us the inequity and hardships they face when they join monolingual classrooms. We see that they are too often viewed only as learners of the classroom language. Their home language and literacy skills often remain overlooked and unrecognized. They are at risk of losing their home language, feelings of loneliness and uncertainty lead them to silence, and they try to hide all traces of their home languages.

With our new understanding of the language lives of immigrant children, we now turn our attention to how we work with them in the classroom. The next chapter explores current classroom practices adopted by EC practitioners and proposes a new, research-based approach that takes the two-sided language lives of young immigrant children into account.

Key Points

1. A language portrait of immigrant children includes their linguistic experiences, skills, strengths, capabilities, and challenges.
2. The purpose of the language portrait is to help EC practitioners understand the language lives of immigrant children.
3. The language portrait shows us that immigrant children
   - are emergent bilinguals,
   - have language lives beyond the classroom,
   - can successfully navigate two languages,
   - have dual language and literacy needs,
   - risk losing their home languages,
   - experience isolation and loneliness,
   - experience language shock and remain silent, and
   - often hide their home languages.
4. The following seven principles are central to understanding childhood bilingualism:
   - Second language learning is not a simple soaking-up process.
   - Young children learn their second language in many different ways.

- Learning the new language involves acquiring skills on two levels: social and academic.
- The two languages of a bilingual work together.
- The home language affects children's personal, social, linguistic, and cognitive development.
- There are cognitive and language processing advantages to bilingualism.
- Language mixing is common and natural in bilinguals.

5. The language and literacy needs of immigrant children go beyond learning the classroom language. In addition to learning their new language, they need to develop their home languages.

6. Daily exposure to the classroom language too often results in the loss of immigrant children's home languages.

7. Entry into a new language environment can result in immigrant children's isolation and loneliness.

8. Referring to the silence of newly arrived immigrant children as transitional behaviour or as the first stage of their classroom language learning is inaccurate and personally and socially damaging. In reality, these children are silenced by the monolingual classroom agenda.

Group Activities

1. Italian Only—No English Allowed!

In this activity, try to imagine what it is like to be in an environment where you do not speak the language and you cannot use the language you know.

> SI PARLA SOLO ITALIANO!

You and a travelling companion (monolingual speakers of English) are travelling through Italy. You drive into a small village and decide to stop for lunch. You see a restaurant with a lovely terrace, and, to your joy, it is not only open for business, but the smells tell you that good things are being prepared in the kitchen. You sit at a table with a red and white chequered tablecloth and pick up the menu. It's all in Italian! There is no English translation like in the restaurants of Rome, Venice, and Florence. You then notice a sign on the wall (see top right). Your uneasiness builds and you wonder what is going to happen. The waiter comes to greet you. A flood of Italian pours from his lips, he points to the menu, smiles, and leaves. You return to the menu and say to your travelling companion, "Now what do we do? I'm starved. Do you recognize any of the words?" After about 10 minutes, the waiter returns, says something very cordially, takes out his pad and pencil, and waits for your order.

Questions for Group Discussion

What would you do?
How would you feel?
How would you communicate that you would like to start lunch with a salad and a glass of red wine?

2. Who Are Immigrant Children?

Working on your own, list the terms you use when referring to immigrant children.
Share your list with your colleagues.
Discuss the limitations of using labels that focus on the classroom language.

3. Newcomers

Working on your own, reflect on the immigrant children who recently arrived in your classroom.
How did they behave? How did their classmates respond?
What do you think happens in the minds of newly arrived immigrant children?
Share your ideas with your colleagues.

CHAPTER 3

CLASSROOM PRACTICES WITH YOUNG IMMIGRANT CHILDREN

The previous chapter helped us understand the linguistic reality and bilingual potential of immigrant children. In this chapter, we will look at how EC practitioners work with these children. We review selected Canadian, American, and European publications that address classroom practices with linguistically diverse children. We then look at how EC practitioners describe their work with immigrant children. Classroom practices are summarized, areas of concern are identified, and a new way of working with young immigrant children is proposed.

"... teachers' understanding of ... language minority students greatly impacts whether these children will be able to walk in two worlds or whether they will experience one set of knowledge, beliefs, and cultural practices imposed on them through hegemonic[1] relationships in the classroom." *(Stebih, 2003, p. 29)*

The reviewed publications include

- Four books (Ashworth & Wakefield, 2004; Kenner, 2000; Nemeth, 2009; Tabors, 2008);
- Two Ontario government early childhood reports, *Supporting English Language Learners in Kindergarten: A Practical Guide for Ontario Educators* (Ontario Ministry of Education, 2007) and *Early Learning for Every Child Today: A Framework for Ontario Early Childhood Settings* (Ontario Ministry of Children and Youth Services, 2007);
- One American document, *Developmentally Appropriate Practice* (National Association for Early Childhood Education, 2009);
- Three European reports, the *Child Immigration Project: Final Report* (Collicelli, 2001), *Integrating Immigrant Children into Schools in Europe* (Eurydice, 2009), and *The Children That Europe Forgot* (Papademetriou & Weidenfeld, 2007); and

- Articles in two early childhood journals: *Young Children* (2001–2010) and *Canadian Children* (2001–2010).[1]

These publications were selected because they are recent and directly address classroom practices as they relate to young immigrant children. Although limited in number, they are representative of current practices on two continents.

> Q: What do the reviewed publications tell us about working with young immigrant children?
> A: The reviewed publications tell us that three different kinds of classroom practices are currently used with immigrant children: assimilative, supportive, and inclusive.

Working with Young Immigrant Children: Current Classroom Practices

Three different kinds of classroom practices emerged from the review of publications (see Figure 3.1). These practices differed in two aspects: the attention paid to the classroom language and the support provided to children's home languages and cultures.

Assimilative practices have a monolingual and monocultural focus; they aim to absorb immigrant children into the majority culture and require them to adopt the societal language, customs, and values. Supportive practices—also referred to as "intercultural"—go one step beyond the teaching of the classroom language. They recognize and value cultural and linguistic differences and acknowledge the importance of home languages. Unlike assimilative and supportive practices, inclusive classroom practices have a multilingual and multi-literate focus, and they bring home languages directly and daily into the classroom. In adopting inclusive practices, EC practitioners promote bilingualism and bi-literacy, work closely with families, and support immigrant children as they navigate and reconcile their two languages and cultures.

1 The number of entries dealing with immigrant children in these two journals in a 10-year span was minimal. For example, between 2001 and 2010, there were 1,134 entries in *Young Children*. Of these, 21 (or 2 per cent) dealt with immigrant children, and 16 (1 per cent) looked at classroom practices. The picture for *Canadian Children* is slightly better. Between 2001 and 2010, there were 171 entries. Of these, 8 (or 5 per cent) dealt with immigrant children and 6 (or 3 per cent) dealt with classroom practices.

FIGURE 3.1: Current Classroom Practices with Young Immigrant Children

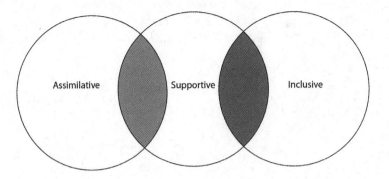

Although the three kinds of classroom practices appear to be separate and mutually exclusive, they are not. The shaded areas of Figure 3.1 show that there is overlap between them. For example, in some accounts found in the publications, assimilative practices included a number of supportive strategies. In the same way, some assimilative strategies were included in supportive practices. Similar overlap was found between the supportive and inclusive practices. However, overlap was *not* found between the two kinds of classroom practices that are starkly different, assimilative and inclusive.

Table 3.1 outlines the main features and the foci for assimilative, supportive and inclusive practices, with examples taken directly from the reviewed publications.

Current Research on Classroom Practices

TABLE 3.1: Classroom Practices with Young Immigrant Children

CLASSROOM PRACTICES		
ASSIMILATIVE	**SUPPORTIVE**	**INCLUSIVE**
MAIN FEATURES ▪ Immigrant children are absorbed into the majority language and culture.	▪ Teaching and learning the classroom language is a priority. ▪ The importance of home languages is acknowledged. ▪ Cultural differences are celebrated.	▪ Home languages are included in the curriculum. ▪ All children experience linguistic diversity. ▪ EC practitioners work closely with families to promote bilingualism and bi-literacy.

CLASSROOM PRACTICES		
ASSIMILATIVE	**SUPPORTIVE**	**INCLUSIVE**
FOCUS Monolingual, mono-literate, and monocultural	Monolingual, mono-literate, and intercultural	Multilingual, multi-literate, and multicultural
STRATEGIES <ul><li>Start Early Project: immerse immigrant children (2–3 years old) into the majority language.</li><li>Provide majority language classes to preschool-aged children.</li><li>Test oral proficiency in the majority language before school entry.</li><li>Provide immigrant children with more face-to-face contact hours with classroom teachers.</li><li>Ground immigrant children in the majority language.</li><li>Limit the proportion of immigrant pupils in mainstream classrooms to one-fifth.</li><li>Separate immigrant children who speak the same language.</li></ul>	<ul><li>Provide home language instruction for those children who will be returning to their country of origin.</li><li>Learn keywords in children's home languages to ease communication.</li><li>Teach the classroom language and celebrate home languages.</li><li>Build relations with families by translating information about the school system into home languages and use interpreters to ease communication.</li><li>Hire resource persons to welcome, guide, and support immigrant families.</li><li>Organize multicultural activities that include all children.</li><li>Transition children into the new language environment.</li></ul>	<ul><li>Have children teach each other to count from 1 to 10 in their home languages.</li><li>EC practitioners who speak immigrant children's home languages use those languages in the classroom.</li><li>Invite parents to read dual language books with the children.</li><li>Use home language literacy materials in the classroom.</li><li>Talk with children about language similarities and differences.</li><li>Learn and use keywords in the home language of each child.</li><li>Display multilingual signs in the classroom.</li></ul>

Assimilative and Supportive Classroom Practices

Assimilative and supportive practices, with their focus on classroom language teaching and learning, stand in contrast to what current research has established about children's dual language learning. These practices rest on the following three erroneous and outdated assumptions about children's dual language learning:

- Children can manage only one language at a time.
- They need to learn their new language as quickly as possible.
- The more time children spend hearing and speaking the classroom language, the better and faster they will master it.

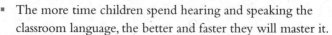

Assimilative and supportive practices short-change immigrant children's language and literacy learning in four ways.

1. They discount their home language and literacy experiences.
2. They define their language needs in terms of learning the classroom language.
3. They fail to use the language resources of EC practitioners effectively.
4. They address only one dimension of immigrant children's cultures.

Each of these four shortcomings is addressed separately.

Assimilative and Supportive Classroom Practices Discount Immigrant Children's Home Language and Literacy Experiences

Information gathered over the years through my research, teaching, and community involvement (see, for example, Chumak-Horbatsch, 2004, 2006, 2008) confirms Goodwin's statement (see text box) and shows that a great deal happens with language and literacy in the homes of many immigrant children. Recall the characterization of their language and literacy lives described in the language portrait (Chapter 2). Classroom practices focused primarily on learning the classroom language, then, disregard and deny immigrant children's home language and literacy lives and send the following messages:

> "... these youngsters not only bring many different skills, strengths, and needs, but also represent unique histories, cultures, stories, values languages, and beliefs."
> (Goodwin, 2002, p. 167)

- My language does not matter here.
- This is a one-language zone.
- The new language is far more important than the language I speak at home.
- If I learn the classroom language, I will make friends and be accepted.

That imigrant children rapidly internalize these messages is evident when we consider the story of Deepta and Maha.

TAMIL IS FOR OUR HOME

Two seven-year-old girls, Deepta and Maha, are speaking Tamil in the playground. When I walk up to them, they suddenly stop talking. I ask them why they have stopped talking, and Maha looks at me and says, "Because we're talking Tamil but we're at school." "Why shouldn't you speak Tamil at school?" I ask. And Deepta replies, "Because Tamil is for our home."

Assimilative and Supportive Classroom Practices Define the Language and Literacy Needs of Immigrant Children in Terms of the Classroom Language

Immigrant children walk and grow in two (or more) language worlds (see Figure 3.2). In their homes, neighbourhoods, and communities, they are exposed to their home language (or languages). In the classroom, they are immersed in a new language. Their language and literacy needs, then, must be understood and defined in terms of the two (or more) languages they experience and learn. Attention paid only to the classroom language devalues their home languages and can negatively affect their developing sense of identity.

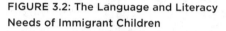

FIGURE 3.2: The Language and Literacy Needs of Immigrant Children

home language(s) and literacy ➡   ⬅ classroom language and literacy

Assimilative and Supportive Classroom Practices Fail to Use the Language Resources of EC Practitioners

In an environment that focuses on learning the classroom language, EC practitioners who speak heritage languages too often hesitate or are unwilling to use these languages with children. This reluctance means that the many benefits of child-staff language match are lost. These benefits include establishing continuity between the home and the classroom, providing an emotionally secure environment for children, reinforcing the importance of home languages and literacies, and providing immigrant children with an out-of-home language model. We will return to this topic in Chapter 6.

The Intercultural Component of Supportive Classroom Practices Addresses Only One Dimension of Immigrant Children's Cultures

The intercultural component of supportive practices too frequently highlights cultural differences in celebratory, entertaining ways that tend to minimize their significance and often amount to tokenism. For example, cultural objects, music, costumes, and food are described, displayed, shared, and celebrated. This part-time attention addresses cultural issues in relation to special days, is devoid of context, and captures only one aspect of the many cultural experiences of immigrant children. To be effective and inclusive, the recognition of cultural diversity should go beyond displays and celebrations. It should engage families and communities and become a substantial part of the classroom curriculum. We will return to this topic in Chapter 7.

Inclusive Classroom Practices

Only inclusive practices, with their multilingual, multi-literate, and multicultural focus and their promotion of bilingualism are in line with the current research-based principles of children's dual language learning summarized here:

- Young children exposed to two rich language environments can manage and separate their two languages.
- Home languages are important for children's overall development.
- Children's development in the home language is a strong predictor of their development in the classroom language.
- Well-developed home language and literacy skills help children acquire literacy and academic language skills in the classroom language.
- The promotion of home languages and literacies in the classroom helps children develop bilingual and bi-literate skills.
- Bilingualism has positive effects on children's personal, social, cognitive, and linguistic development.
- The focus on learning the classroom language in the early years can negatively affect immigrant children's overall development, resulting in the loss of home languages and weakened family communication dynamics.

For more information on childhood bilingualism, see Baker (2006), Bialystok (1987a, 1987b, 1997, 2001a, 2001b), Chang (1993), Cummins (2001a, 2001b), Genesee (2008), Genesee, Paradis, and Crago (2010), Nemeth (2009), and Wong Fillmore (1991).

To summarize, the review of the selected publications revealed three different kinds of practices adopted with young immigrant children: assimilative, supportive, and inclusive. Inclusive practices match established principles of childhood bilingualism, while assimilative and supportive practices rest on erroneous and outdated second language learning principles. As well, the intercultural focus of supportive practices is one sided and falls short of capturing the cultural lives of immigrant children. We now look at how EC practitioners describe their work with immigrant children.

Working with Immigrant Children: Reports from EC Practitioners

Three recent studies documented the classroom practices of EC practitioners who work with immigrant children. In the Childcare Study (Chumak-Horbatsch, 2010), 225 supervisors (with a total of 2,822 staff members) completed an online survey on how their staff work with immigrant children. The survey included multiple-choice questions about classroom practices. Even though the survey did not allow respondents to provide comments or additional information, the responses paint a fairly accurate picture of the practices used with young children who come from homes where heritage languages are spoken and whose understanding of the classroom language is minimal.

> Q: Which classroom practices do EC practitioners adopt in their work with immigrant children?
>
> A: For the most part, EC practitioners adopt supportive classroom practices: they focus on immigrant children's mastery of the classroom language, acknowledge the importance of home languages, and support and celebrate cultural diversity. In addition to these strategies, they adopt some assimilative and inclusive practices.

All childcare centre supervisors reported that staff helped immigrant children in three ways: settle into the classroom, make friends, and learn the classroom language. EC practitioners also recognized the importance of home languages, learned and used key words and phrases in children's home languages to ease communication, celebrated cultures, and welcomed families into the classroom.

Many of these practices were noted in two other studies. Pacini-Ketchabaw (2007) found that in Victoria and Vancouver, two Canadian cities with large immigrant populations, EC practitioners focused on helping immigrant children learn the classroom language as quickly as possible and paid little attention to their home languages: "immigrant children require more work and attention from the educators because of ... English development" (p. 227–228). In a similar way, EC practitioners at a North Carolina childcare centre focused on immigrant children's learning of English: "they really want them to learn English" (Hardin et al., 2010, p. 31). They reported that working with children and families who have limited proficiency in the classroom language was problematic: "It's frustrating on my part because I can't get them to understand what I'm saying" (p. 31). At the same time, these EC practitioners reported that home languages were important, and, like their Toronto counterparts, they learned and used key words and phrases in home languages to communicate with immigrant children.

To summarize, the EC practitioners who reported on their work with immigrant children adopted different kinds of classroom practices. Assimilative practices, such as hurrying immigrant children into the classroom language, and inclusive practices, such as pairing children and staff who speak the same heritage languages, were reported infrequently. However, supportive practices, in other words, focusing on the classroom language and paying symbolic attention to home languages and cultures, were reported most often.

Where Do We Go from Here?

Before we consider the next step, let's pause here to review our discussion of classroom practices with young immigrant children:

1. We identified three different kinds of classroom practices adopted with young immigrant children: assimilative, supportive, and inclusive.
2. We saw that assimilative and supportive classroom practices short-change immigrant children's language and literacy learning, rest on erroneous and outdated assumptions about children's dual language learning, and do not meet the language and literacy needs of immigrant children.
3. We also saw that inclusive classroom practices, with their multilingual and multi-literacy focus and their promotion of bilingualism, meet the language and literacy needs of immigrant children and are in line with research-based principles of dual language learning.
4. For the most part, EC practitioners adopt supportive practices. These focus on the learning and teaching of the classroom language, acknowledge the importance of home languages, and support and celebrate cultural diversity.
5. Assimilative and inclusive classroom practices were minimally adopted by EC practitioners.

The Next Step

TABLE 3.2: Moving from Monolingual to Multilingual Classroom Practices

WHERE ARE WE NOW?	WHERE DO WE WANT TO BE?
MONOLINGUAL CLASSROOM PRACTICES	**MULTILINGUAL CLASSROOM PRACTICE**
Assimilative Practices Supportive Practices	Linguistically Appropriate Practice
▪ Fail to meet the dual language and literary needs of young immigrant children. ▪ Rest on erroneous and outdated assumptions about children's language learning.	▪ Meets the dual language and literacy needs of young immigrant children. ▪ Rests on research-based principles of children's language learning. ▪ Builds on and extends inclusive classroom practices.

Now, with our new understanding of current classroom practices, we are ready to do two things: review our own work with immigrant children and consider moving toward multilingual practices (see Table 3.2).

The right side of Table 3.2 shows an alternative to monolingual practices. "Linguistically Appropriate Practice" or LAP is a new, inclusive way of working with young immigrant children. Built on inclusive practices, LAP directly addresses the dual language and literacy needs of immigrant children, welcomes all languages into the classroom, and provides enriching language and literacy experiences for *all* children. In the next chapter, we begin our exploration of LAP.

Key Points

1. A review of selected Canadian, American, and European publications revealed three different kinds of classroom practices currently adopted by EC practitioners in their work with young immigrant children: assimilative, supportive, and inclusive.

2. Assimilative practices absorb immigrant children into the classroom language and culture. Supportive practices focus on learning the classroom language, recognize and value cultural and linguistic differences, and acknowledge home languages. Inclusive practices bring home languages into the classroom and promote multilingualism and multi-literacy.

3. There is some overlap between (a) assimilative and supportive and (b) supportive and inclusive classroom practices, but assimilative and

inclusive practices do not overlap.

4. Assimilative and supportive classroom practices do not meet the language and literacy needs of young immigrant children. They rest on erroneous and outdated assumptions, including the idea that young children can manage only one language at a time.

5. Inclusive practices are in line with current research that describes immigrant children as capable, active dual language learners.

6. In their work with immigrant children, EC practitioners mostly adopt supportive classroom practices and minimally adopt assimilative and inclusive practices.

7. "Linguistically Appropriate Practice" or LAP is proposed as a new way to work with young immigrant children. LAP builds on inclusive classroom practices, is in line with the principles of childhood bilingualism, and meets the language and literacy needs of immigrant children.

Group Activities

1. Understanding the Immigrant Experience

Choose one or more books about the experience of immigrant children from the list found in Appendix 3.A. With your colleagues, think of different ways you can use these books with families and with children.

2. My Classroom Practices

The following questions will serve as a guide in your discussion about classroom practices:

- How would you define the language and literacy needs of young immigrant children?
- Which kinds of classroom practices do you currently adopt in your work with immigrant children? (Refer to Table 3.1: Classroom Practices with Young Immigrant Children.)
- How much of your work with immigrant children is assimilative? Supportive? Inclusive?
- With your colleagues, discuss the shortcomings of assimilative and supportive classroom practices. Why is it important to move from monolingual to multilingual classroom practices?

APPENDIX 3.A

Books about Newcomer Arrival and Adjustment

Aliki. 1999. *Marianthe's story*. New York: Greenwillow Books.

Ashley, B. 1993. *Cleversticks*. New York: Harper Collins.

Bunting, E. 2006. *One green apple*. New York: Clarion Books.

Carden, M., & Cappellini, M. (eds.). 1997. *I am of two places: Children's poetry*. Crystal Lake, IL: Rigby.

Choi, Y. 2001. *The name jar*. New York: Alfred A. Knopf.

English, K. 2000. *Speak English for us, Marisol!* Morton Grove, IL: Albert Whitman.

Garland, S. 1997. *The lotus seed*. San Diego, CA: Harcourt Brace.

Herrera, J.F. 2000. *The upside down boy/El nino de cabeza*. San Francisco, CA: Children's Book Press.

Hoffman, M., & Littlewood, K. 2002. *The colour of home*. London: Frances Lincoln.

Jimenez, F. 1998. *La mariposa*. Boston: Houghton Mifflin.

Khan, R. 2008. *Coming to Canada*. Toronto: Groundwood Books.

Levine, E. 1989. *I hate English!* New York: Scholastic.

Miller, E.I. 1999. *Just like home/Como en mi tierra*. Morton Grove, IL: Albert Whitman.

Mobin-Uddin, A. 2005. *My name is Bilal*. Homesdale, PA: Boyds Mills Press.

Munsch, R.N. 1995. *From far away*. Toronto: Annick Press.

Nobisso, J. 2002. *In English of course*. New York: Gingerbread House.

Pak, S. 2002. *A place to grow*. New York: Scholastic.

Pak, S. 2003. *Sumi's first day of school ever*. New York: Viking.

Park, F., & Park, G. 2002. *Goodbye, 382 Shin Dang Dong*. Washington, DC: National Geographic Society.

Recorvits, H. 2003. *My name is Yoon*. New York: Farrar, Straus and Giroux.

Rosenberg, L. 1999. *The silence in the mountains*. New York: Orchard Books.

Tan, S. 2006. *The arrival*. New York: Arthur A. Levine Books.

Thien, M. 2001. *The Chinese violin*. Vancouver: Whitecap Books.

CHAPTER 4

LINGUISTICALLY APPROPRIATE PRACTICE: BACKGROUND

Let's review what we have learned so far. We saw that immigrant children are a significant presence in the classrooms of urban centres. The language portrait helped us understand these children. We saw that they have bilingual potential and unique language and literacy needs. We also saw that they face challenges in monolingual classrooms. The publication review revealed three approaches to working with immigrant children: assimilative, supportive, and inclusive. Of these, EC practitioners mostly adopt the supportive approach, a monolingual practice that constrains the language and literacy experiences of immigrant children. In the previous chapter, "Linguistically Appropriate Practice" or LAP, a new way of working with immigrant children, was introduced.

> "Knowledge about children's learning is dynamic and childcare workers need to remain informed and respond to incorporating new ideas into their practice rather than to approach their work in a prescriptive way." *(Berthelsen & Brownlee, 2007, p. 360)*

We are now ready to explore LAP. We begin with a definition and explain why a new way of working with immigrant children is needed. We then provide a description of dynamic bilingualism, the theoretical grounding of LAP.

Defining LAP

So what do we mean by "Linguistically Appropriate Practice"? LAP is an inclusive approach to working with immigrant children. It looks at them differently—not simply as learners of the classroom language but as bilinguals in the making. The starting point for LAP is that immigrant children have two language environments—the home and the classroom. As a result, they have dual language and literacy needs. Here is a snapshot definition of LAP.

LAP

- is a new approach to working with immigrant children;
- builds on and extends current inclusive practices;
- views immigrant children as emergent bilinguals, *not* simply as learners of the classroom language;
- acknowledges immigrant children's dual language and literacy needs;
- builds partnerships with families;
- recognizes the importance of home languages;
- links children's home and classroom language and literacy experiences;
- builds on children's home language and literacy experiences;
- promotes bilingualism;
- encourages home language use in the classroom;
- encourages "translanguaging"[1] or the use of two or more languages;
- helps *all* children experience, understand, and accept linguistic diversity; and
- is designed to help prepare children for the complex communication and literacy demands of the 21st century.

Why Do We Need LAP?

There are three reasons why we need clear, practical guidelines for working with young immigrant children.

First, current policy documents and curriculum guidelines, for the most part, pay little attention to the language and literacy needs of young immigrant children. Their focus can best be described as "supportive," as they pay particular attention to teaching the classroom language and offer minimal acknowledgement of home languages and cultures.[2]

> "We are sort of learning as we go."
> (Pacini-Ketchabaw, 2007, p. 229)

Second, reflecting the approach put forward in policy documents and curriculum guidelines, supportive classroom practices are widely adopted by EC practitioners. However, research has shown that supportive classroom practices do not meet the language and literacy needs of immigrant children.

---

1 See discussion in section "Languaging and Translanguaging."

2 A recent example can be found in the *Early Years Study 3*, a Canadian policy document that outlines the current state of Canadian families with young children and provides the social, economic, and scientific rationale for increased public investments in early childhood education (McCain, Mustard, & McCuaig, 2011).

Finally, because the discussion of the language and literacy needs of immigrant children in policy documents and curriculum guidelines is superficial, at best, many professionals (EC practitioners, family resource staff, speech and language pathologists, settlement workers, in-service teachers, and school principals), unsure of what "works best" with immigrant children, have requested guidance.[1]

> "We hear a lot about inclusion, in relation to children with special needs, but nothing about language inclusion." *(EC practitioner working with preschoolers)*

Dynamic Bilingualism—Much More Than Just Adding a Language

LAP is grounded in dynamic bilingualism (García, 2009a, 2009c), a theory that focuses on languages that speakers *use* rather than on separate languages they *have*. García defines dynamic bilingualism as "language practices that are multiple and ever adjusting to the multilingual multimodal terrain of the communicative act" (García, 2009a, p. 144). How is this view different from the way we normally look at bilingualism?

In 1975, Lambert proposed two kinds of bilingualism: subtractive and additive. In subtractive bilingualism (illustrated as $L_1 + L_2 - L_1 = L_2$), mastery of the second language (L_2), which is the dominant language of a society, occurs at the price of losing the first language (L_1), the language of the home. The result is a monolingual speaker. In additive bilingualism (illustrated as $L_1 + L_2 = L_1 + L_2$), the dominant language (L_2) is added to the home language (L_1), resulting in mastery of two separate languages with two sets of skills. The result is viewed as a form of double monolingualism.

In subtractive and additive bilingualism, language is treated "outside and beyond human beings" (Yngve, 1996, p. 28) and is not necessarily linked to the way people actually *use* language. This static and linear approach to language represents a monolingual reality in which the two languages of a bilingual speaker are seen as separate entities that are not linked to one another in any way. However, we know that language is a fluid social behaviour that cannot be studied without reference to its speakers, their distinct and varied language practices, and the many contexts in which they use language. In other words, language is not separate from how people simply "language."

---

1 In my interactions with professionals over the years, I have received numerous requests for guidance and direction in working with immigrant children.

The linear, traditional models of additive and subtractive bilingualism have been described as inadequate, insufficient, and unworkable in the twenty-first century. The increased movement of people, information, services, and goods means that communication is more complex and is accompanied by a new awareness of languages (García, 2009a, 2009c). Communication technology and globalization have significantly changed and extended the ways in which languages are used. As information is readily accessed in a number of different languages and as communication becomes multilingual and occurs in various contexts with a multitude of speakers in different parts of the globe, using a vast array of technologies and media, bilingualism (or, increasingly, multilingualism) becomes a dynamic and important resource.

"What is different today from the ways in which people languaged in the 19th and 20th centuries is that we can simultaneously and collaboratively engage in many different language practices at the same time, as happens in electronic instant messaging and chatting." *(García, 2009c, p. 29)*

In response to these global and technological changes, García proposes dynamic bilingualism, which focuses on the social and communicative aspects of the languages that bilinguals encounter—on language practice or actual language use and *not* on learning specific language skills. Dynamic bilingualism, García explains, is not about adding a second language. It is about using one's entire linguistic repertoire to deal with communication circumstances or "developing complex language practices that encompass several social contexts" (García, 2010, p. 196).

Figure 4.1 illustrates the multi-directionality of dynamic bilingualism. The multidirectional arrows—some straight, others curved, some blank, others shaded—represent the many languages, communication contexts, and language practices required to navigate a multilingual world. García refers to dynamic bilingualism as a twenty-first century "necessity" that reflects the complexities of communication in our global world.

FIGURE 4.1: Dynamic Bilingualism

Source: García and Kleifgen (2010, p. 44).

For a detailed discussion of how globalization affects language practice, see García (2009c).

Language Ecology

Dynamic bilingualism represents a language ecology perspective—a multilingual orientation that takes into consideration all language circumstances, contexts, and speakers. The term "language ecology" is defined by Norwegian linguist Einar Haugen (1972) as "the study of interactions between any given language and its environment" (p. 343). Language ecology challenges the monolingual ideology and order and rejects the idea that language is an "isolated, self-contained system" defined by rule learning and usage (Kramsch & Steffensen, 2008, p. 18). Proponents argue that natural interactions in everyday surroundings, both personal and sociocultural, make language happen. Language ecology highlights diversity; "stands up for the minority language and its learners"; encourages the creation of multilingual environments where many different languages exist, develop, and grow; and pays special attention to marginal and fragile language circumstances (Kramsch & Steffensen, 2008, p. 20).

Creese and Martin (2006) suggest that understanding language ecology is important and useful for educators. By thinking of their classrooms as "linguistically complex ecosystems," they will better understand the changing language lives (development, abilities, relationships, attitudes, losses, gains) of the children, be mindful of their language practices, and be aware of the fact that, as in biological ecosystems, any change, focus, or influence, however subtle, will in some way affect children's language lives. This is "healthy and good" for both the classroom environment and the wider majority ideological orientations about linguistic diversity.

Languaging and Translanguaging

The term "languaging" describes language as an action. It takes into consideration what speakers actually *do* with language (García, 2010, p. 194). To "language" means to use language alone, to share it with others, to solve problems, and to create and shape (or reshape) meanings and understandings. García argues that referring to the "languaging" of bilinguals is more accurate than considering the skills they have mastered in each of their languages.

She goes on to say that bilinguals "language" differently than monolinguals because they adjust their language practices in multiple and mixed contexts and naturally move between their languages. What they do, then, is "translanguage." The term *trawsieithu* or "translanguaging" was first used by Cen Williams to describe a teaching methodology adopted in Welsh-English bilingual classrooms to strengthen and develop children's dual language listening, speaking, reading, and writing (cited in Baker, 2006). García extends the original meaning of translanguaging to include all bilinguals, reminding us that this is the communicative norm of dual language speakers and communities throughout the world (García 2009c, p. 43).

As they translanguage, bilinguals make use of multiple communicative possibilities, practices, and choices. They use their languages flexibly, shifting, mixing, and blending linguistic features. They go back and forth from one language to the other, combining elements from each language to convey their language and social skills and their cultural knowledge and understanding. Far more complex than code-switching, translanguaging involves shifting from one language to another in the course of a conversation. It includes crossing language borders, adjusting and modifying language practice to match changing social and communicative needs—for example, reading in one language and discussing the content in another. These practices facilitate communication and help bilinguals manage their two language worlds.

Dynamic Bilingualism in Action

In her translanguaging study, García (2011) documents the language use of Latino children and their teachers in a Spanish-English bilingual kindergarten program. This is the first study of translanguaging in young bilinguals. Even though five-year-old children were included in a translanguaging study conducted in British complementary schools, where students spoke Gujarati and Mandarin (Creese & Blackledge, 2010), all of the documented examples in this study come from older bilinguals. Wei (2011) also focuses on older bilinguals in her study exploring the translanguaging practices of Chinese university students.

In García's study, the two-way program was "linguistically compartmentalized" or separated into half-day English and half-day Spanish instruction, with classrooms assigned to each language of instruction. The children, however, had a different idea. They created their own "third spaces," engaged in "complex languaging practices," and made flexible use of all of their language strengths and skills. During their free-time (as opposed to instructional-time) interactions, they selected one language over another, mixed languages, translated to and for each other, and engaged in two-language experimentation, integration, and negotiation. Such behaviours, García concludes, helped these bilingual children construct their hybrid linguistic and cultural identities.

Translanguaging, García argues, has "much value" for bilingual children. The opportunity to use home languages in the classroom gives them a voice and builds and capitalizes on their home language practices, allowing them to take ownership of their home language and formulate their personal identities. In addition to supporting these personal gains, classrooms where children's natural language practices are encouraged serve to:

- promote bilingualism,
- reduce language loss,
- value bilingual families and communities,
- recognize home language use as a linguistic human right,
- encourage collaboration among children as they negotiate linguistically,
- help children construct meaning with peers and adults, and
- foster an understanding and acceptance of linguistic differences and language practices.

Summary

LAP is a new classroom practice that extends current inclusive practices and reflects the principles of dynamic bilingualism. Developed in response to the widespread use of monolingual classroom practices, which fall short of meeting the language and literacy needs of immigrant children, and to the numerous requests from EC practitioners for guidance, LAP views immigrant children as emergent bilinguals, acknowledges their unique language and literacy needs, focuses on the social and communicative aspects of languages, encourages translanguaging, promotes bilingualism, and builds partnerships with families.

This chapter brings us to the end of Part I, which lays the groundwork for LAP. We are now ready to move to Part II, which sets the stage for launching this new classroom practice.

Key Points

1. What is LAP? LAP is a new approach to working with immigrant children. Grounded in dynamic bilingualism, LAP views immigrant children as emergent bilinguals, focuses on their dual language and literacy needs, links their home and classroom language and literacy experiences, prepares them for the complex communication and literacy demands of the twenty-first century, and helps all children understand and accept linguistic diversity.
2. Why do we need LAP? Overall, classroom practices do not meet the language and literacy needs of immigrant children. As well, judging by requests for guidance from professionals, clear, practical guidelines for working with immigrant children are needed.

3. Traditional views of bilingualism that separate languages and focus on specific language skills are no longer relevant in our global and technological world.

4. Dynamic bilingualism

- views bilingualism as *dynamic* rather than *linear*;
- represents a response to global and technological communication changes;
- focuses on the social and communicative aspects of language;
- focuses on language practice—on *using* language—and not on specific language skills;
- views bilinguals as users of their languages;
- represents a "language ecology" perspective—a multilingual orientation that takes into consideration all language circumstances, contexts, and speakers and helps EC practitioners better understand children's changing language circumstances by enabling them to view the classroom as a "linguistically complex ecosystem";
- views the bilingual's two languages as part of a continuous bilingual repertoire;
- sees both languages as interactive, complimentary, and dependent on each other;
- suggests that bilinguals "language" differently than monolinguals;
- refers to the language practice of bilinguals as "translanguaging"— which is the flexible use of two languages, shifting, mixing, blending, going back and forth from one language to the other, and combining elements from each language; and
- recognizes that there are personal, social, and communicative benefits for children who translanguage.

Group Activities: Thinking about Bilingualism

This three-part group activity invites EC practitioners to reflect, discuss, and exchange views about bilingualism.

"Reflection is what allows us to learn from our experiences: it is an assessment of where we have been and where we want to go next."
(Wolf, 2002)

1. What Does Bilingualism Mean to Me?

- Take a few minutes to write down, in point form, your own personal definition of bilingualism.
- Compare your definition with those of your colleagues.

- Discuss the similarities and the differences noted in recorded definitions.
- On chart paper, prepare a group definition of bilingualism.

2. My Bilingual Profile

This activity will provide bilingual EC practitioners with the opportunity to reflect on their own language use.

- Include the following in your own personal language use profile: What was my first language; Did I learn a second language? When? Do I translanguage? How often? In which contexts?
- When your language profile is complete, share your responses with your colleagues.

3. Bilingualism in the Twenty-First Century

- Read the section on dynamic bilingualism either individually or as a group.
- Take turns choosing and explaining one highlight of dynamic bilingualism (refer to #4 in the "Key Points" section).
- How do you feel about children using languages you don't understand?

PART II

Setting the Stage for LAP

CHAPTER 5

PREPARING THE CLASSROOM FOR LAP

Our Classroom Is a Place Where Languages Are Welcome

Part I provides us with important information about immigrant children and classroom practices. After reading it, we see that young children from diverse language backgrounds are found in high numbers in Canadian, American, and European classrooms. We understand that current mono-

lingual practices are insufficient and that a new classroom approach, called LAP, is a better fit with what we know about dynamic bilingualism and the language ecology approach to language learning. LAP not only acknowledges the importance of home languages—it brings them right into the classroom and promotes children's bilingualism.

We are now ready to set the stage for LAP. The chapter begins with a challenge, inviting EC practitioners to make a conscious commitment to adopt LAP. Then it provides strategies for preparing a LAP-friendly classroom.

The LAP Challenge

Accepting the LAP challenge is a big step. But what does it really mean? It means that you agree to promote language inclusion, fairness, acceptance, and growth in your classroom. The LAP challenge calls on EC practitioners to:

- refer to and view immigrant children as emergent bilinguals, not simply as learners of the classroom language;
- open their classroom doors to *all* languages;
- encourage immigrant children to translanguage;
- build partnerships with families;
- promote multilingualism and multi-literacy;
- create and sustain a multilingual classroom environment; and
- help *all* children understand and accept language differences.

> "But I don't speak, read, or write Mandarin or Yoruba or Arabic or Tamil!" laments a Grade 2 teacher discussing classroom practices.
>
> Q: Can I promote bilingualism and bi-literacy?
>
> Can I open my classroom door to languages that I don't understand or speak or read or write?
>
> A: YES you can!

The adoption of LAP does not come with unrealistic expectations. It does not require the EC practitioner to become a polyglot[1] or to speak and be literate in the many languages spoken by the children in his or her classroom. What it does require, however, is an understanding of dynamic bilingualism and a readiness to promote bilingualism in a classroom that has been set up to reflect the language backgrounds of the children. For a discussion of how a monolingual EC practitioner can promote bilingualism, see Schwarzer, Haywood, and Lorenzen (2003).

Strategies for Preparing the Classroom for LAP

Classroom Language Policy

A classroom language policy is a set of rules and expectations that guide and direct classroom language use and behaviours. Develop your classroom language policy together with the children. Using the phrase *"Our classroom is a place where languages are …"* as a starting point, discuss and list children's contributions on chart paper. A sample is provided in Figure 5.1. Keep your list age-appropriate, short, and clear. Invite the children, their parents, or others proficient in various languages to translate the classroom language policy into children's home languages. Display the classroom language policy for children, families, staff, and visitors to see.

---

1 A person with a command of many languages.

FIGURE 5.1: Sample Classroom Language Policy

> **OUR CLASSROOM IS A PLACE WHERE LANGUAGES ARE ...**
> welcome   respected   spoken   learned   accepted   compared
> discussed   never forbidden   never laughed at   discovered   written
> read   shared   sung   explored

The Language Survey

Information about home language and literacy use is invaluable to EC practitioners as they link children's home and classroom language environments. The language survey (see Appendix 5.A), presented to parents or guardians at the time of registration, includes questions about home language and literacy practices.

There are, of course, other ways to collect and make use of personal and family information that will help you launch LAP and prepare a multilingual classroom environment. Keep in mind the need for sensitivity and confidentiality when you gather, store, and use this information. Here are some tips:

1. Providing information about home languages is voluntary.
2. Respect and accept parents' unwillingness to provide information.
3. Accept incomplete information.
4. Respect the confidentiality of parents. Never share or discuss collected information with other parents.

Language Charts

Once you learn what languages your children speak at home, invite them and their parents to prepare a chart for their home language. The "Language Chart Template" shows the features to include. Encourage the parents and children to add features that are special to their countries of origin, such as celebratory days, instruments, flowers, and animals. Don't forget to prepare a chart for the societal languages, English and French.

LANGUAGE CHART TEMPLATE
Name of language:
Speakers in our class:
(a) Number
(b) Names
Spoken in these countries:
Flag:
Writing system, e.g., directionality (left to right, right to left), characters or letters:
Counting system:

The following websites provide information about the main languages of the world and will help in the preparation of your language charts:

- http://www.irb-cisr.gc.ca:8080/Publications/index_e.aspx (Immigration and Refugee Board of Canada's *National Documentation Packages, Issue Papers, and Country Fact Sheets*)
- http://en.wikipedia.org/wiki/Countries_of_the_world (Wikipedia's *List of Sovereign States*).
- http://www.123world.com/languages/ (*123World: Languages*)
- http://www.ethnologue.com/web.asp (*Ethnologue: Languages of the World*)

Display the language chart in the classroom. In an age-appropriate way, discuss language similarities and differences with the children. Parents can be invited to join these discussions and to explain the highlights of their home languages.

The Language Centre—A Place Where Languages Come to Life

The language centre is an interest and exploration classroom area where children, EC practitioners, and parents can

- discover, share, compare, use, and learn languages;
- translanguage;
- share books in different languages;
- write and count in different languages; and
- sing, listen to music, and share songs in different languages.

Getting Started

Select a classroom area for the language centre. Include the following in the language centre:

- a table for four to six children;
- a chart stand and a display board;
- a listening station (headphones, cassette recorder, CDs, DVDs)
- writing instruments (markers, crayons, pencils);
- coloured and white, lined and unlined paper of different sizes and textures;
- books in different languages;
- a world map and a globe; and
- a computer.

Language Centre Schedule

Schedule daily language centre time with the class—approximately 10 minutes with younger children and 15 minutes with older ones. Mornings work best, when children are ready for reflective, engaging activities. Encourage families to join in language centre activities and share their skills and knowledge. Parents and grandparents can participate in small group activities or work with individual children in the language centre. Details of parental participation are included with the activities described in Chapter 7.

Introducing the Language Centre to the Children

In an age-appropriate way, explain the wonder and importance of human speech to the children. Refer to the language fact sheet found in Appendix 5.B.

Point out the languages spoken by the children and adults in the classroom. Tell the children that, as a group, the class will be spending some time every day in the language centre, talking and learning about languages and reading and singing in different languages. Remind the children that they are free to visit the language centre during self-selected activity time. Together with the children, plan, prepare, and display a language centre sign.

Classroom Set-Up

The physical set-up of a classroom is important. All the physical elements—pictures, signs, displays, colours, patterns, the arrangement of objects, books, furniture, lighting, and sounds—reflect program highlights and priorities, send messages to families and visitors, and influence children's thinking and sense of awareness. It is important to remember that omissions also send messages. The suggestions that follow will help the EC practitioner create a physical space that tells children, families, and visitors how important their languages and cultures are in the classroom.

THE LAP CLASSROOM SAYS...

Everyone is welcome here.
There is a place here for all languages.
Languages matter.

Multilingual Signs

Signs in home languages send a welcoming, inclusive message. They link home and classroom and create a supportive visual environment. Basic multilingual signs are large-sized posters depicting a wide range of topics and concepts such as greetings, farewells, holidays, activities, numbers, months, days of the week, simple objects, and weather words or labels. The two following websites offer multilingual signs for purchase or for downloading as bulletin board printables. These signs can be used as templates, and, with the help of the Language Committee,[1] can be translated into home languages.

- http://www.schoolslinks.co.uk/resources_dl.htm
- http://www.languagelizard.com/Number-Cards-10-100-Multilingual-Edition-p/frnumb100.htm

Engage children and families in the preparation and display of the multilingual classroom signs. Take the time to discuss their purpose and content. Be sure to change classroom signs regularly to ensure that they do not turn into classroom fixtures that go unnoticed.

Displaying Children's Work

Displaying children's work—such as labelled artwork, dual language books, word cards, and stories—will reflect the multilingual and multi-literate character of your classroom. Some of the activities described in Chapter 7 can be displayed in the classroom.

Book Displays

Displaying books in home languages and books with bilingual texts (dual language books) is common practice in classrooms with immigrant children. However, these books too often remain on the bookshelf for long periods of time and go unnoticed by the children. For this reason, it is a good idea to separate classroom books by language. Suggestions for sorting and colour-coding classroom books can be found in Chapter 7.

Housekeeping Centre

A simple and inexpensive way to create a multilingual classroom is to ask the children to bring containers and packaging (tins, cartons, bags, plastic bottles) of their favourite foods and household items from home. Following a safety check to remove sharp edges and metal parts, place the containers in the housekeeping centre for children's exploration and experimentation. At regular intervals, discard torn and worn containers and request new contributions to keep the housekeeping centre supply abundant and sturdy.

---

1 See Chapter 6 for a discussion of the parent group called the "Language Committee."

Plan a discussion about the main features of the containers: name, languages on the labels, purpose (eat, clean, wash, wear, or play), and country of origin. Encourage the children to explain where the items were purchased and what they are used for.

Classroom News Board

Create a classroom news board where you post monthly or weekly schedules, plans, and events. Invite parents to post family-friendly events taking place in the community.

Multilingual Music in the Classroom

In their homes and communities, most children are exposed to music that is specific to their cultures. They may be familiar with or play specialized instruments, and they may have witnessed and participated in singing in their home

> "Listening to music all over the planet ... fosters an open ear and an open mind. Learning to hear a strange music from the viewpoint of the people who make that music enlarges our understanding and increases our pleasure."
> *(Titon, 2009, p. 5)*

languages. Bringing these musical experiences into the classroom involves more than simply turning on a CD for background music. It requires careful planning and the help of parents.

Classroom Multilingual Music Library

Ask parents to donate instrumental or vocal CDs to create a classroom music library. Be sure to include the home languages of EC practitioners. Using coloured stickers that correspond to the classroom language colour codes,[1] label each CD and store them in a sturdy box. Invite the children to prepare a multilingual sign for the classroom CD collection.

Classroom Music Schedule

Create a music schedule that indicates who is responsible for playing music each week. The schedule should show the home languages, the names of speakers of those languages, and the dates during which each group of speakers is responsible for playing music (see Table 5.1 for a sample schedule). For one week, the children who are speakers of a particular language will select and insert CDs into the player.

---

1 See Chapter 7 for colour coding the classroom.

TABLE 5.1: Sample Classroom Music Schedule

LANGUAGE	DATE	SPEAKERS
English	March 7 to 11	Miss Ross, Elizabeth, Joshua
Mandarin	March 14 to 18	Huan, Lin, Shan, Miss Pearl
Arabic	March 21 to 25	Amira, Baraka, Akbar
Urdu	March 28 to April 1	Johara, Sabirah, Tahir
Polish	April 4 to 8	Agnieczka
Farsi	April 11 to 15	Ali, Sadri, Karim, Azin, Navid

TIPS

- Play the music several times during the day: arrival, nap or rest time, snack time, child-directed activity time, and dismissal.
- Talk to the children about the different kinds of music, for example, instrumental, vocal, classical, jazz, pop, and rap. Use samples to illustrate your discussion.

Summary

The suggestions provided in this chapter will help you set the stage for LAP. They include taking the LAP challenge, developing and promoting a classroom language policy, collecting and posting information on the home languages and cultures of the people in your classroom, setting up a language centre, and filling your classroom with multilingual signs, books, objects, and music. If you follow these suggestions, a visitor looking in your open classroom door will quickly see and hear that you have created a multilingual environment where languages matter. In the next chapter, we will address four topics that will help us launch LAP.

Key Points

1. The EC practitioner who takes the LAP challenge agrees to promote language inclusion, fairness, acceptance, and growth.
2. Monolingual EC practitioners can readily promote bilingualism.
3. A classroom language policy is a set of rules and expectations that guide and direct classroom language use and behaviours.
4. Information about home language use is invaluable to EC practitioners as they link the children's home and classroom language and literacy experiences.

5. Collecting information about children's home languages and literacy behaviours should be conducted in a professional manner.
6. Home language charts will help all children understand linguistic diversity and will serve as a link between the home and the classroom.
7. The language centre is a classroom space where languages come to life.
8. The physical set-up of the classroom is important. LAP can best happen in an environment filled with multilingual signs, displays, books, and music.

Group Activities

1. Taking the LAP Challenge

LAP starts with a willingness on your part to take the challenge, to try something important and different.

- Ask yourself whether you are ready to take the LAP challenge.
- Are you prepared to open your classroom door to all languages?
- How do you feel when you hear languages you do not understand?
- Reflect on what these feelings mean in terms of your attitude toward the language and literacy learning of immigrant children.

2. Home Language Charts

Set aside a time to share resources and prepare home language charts together with your colleagues.

(a) Compare the language backgrounds of children across groups or classrooms.

(b) Plan activities across classrooms, so children who speak the same home languages will have opportunities to use these languages at school.

3. Is My Classroom a Multilingual Environment?

Think of ways to "multi-lingualize" your classroom. Look over the suggestions found in this chapter and begin to transform your classroom to reflect the home languages of both children and adults.

APPENDIX 5.A

....

Sample Language Survey

....

Note: Use this survey as a guide. Add or delete questions as needed. In this sample survey, "English" is listed as the classroom language. Replacing "your child" with each child's name makes the survey more personal. Add a note reassuring parents that the information they provide will be treated with confidentiality.

1. Child's name: _____

2 Age: _____ Date of birth: _____

3. Country of birth: _____

4. Names and ages of brothers:

    _____

    _____

5. Names and ages of sisters:

    _____

    _____

6. Home language (or languages): _____

7. Do you have language rules in your home? Are there specific language behaviours expected of your child?   ☐ Yes   ☐ No

8. Please explain.

    _____

9. Do grandparents live in your home?   ☐ Yes   ☐ No

10. If YES, what language or languages do grandparents use with your child:

    _____

11. Do the grandparents speak English?   ☐ Yes   ☐ No

12. How well does your child know the home language?

    _____

13. How much English does your child know?

    _____

14. Which languages or language does your child use at home?

    _____

15. What is your child's stronger or dominant language?

_____

16. Does your child prefer one language to another? Please explain:

_____

17. How many hours per week does your child watch

    English-language TV?   _____

    Home-language TV?   _____

18. Do you read books in the home language to your child? ☐ Yes ☐ No

    If YES, how often?

_____

19. Do you read English language books to your child? ☐ Yes ☐ No

    If YES, how often?

_____

20. Do you have any concerns or questions about your child's language or languages?

_____

21. Does your child enjoy music, singing, or dancing? Please explain.

_____

22. Do you have a house pet? _____

23. Do you visit your country of origin? How often? Do you take your child with you?

_____

24. Please list your child's special interests, talents:

_____

_____

25. Please list any clubs or programs your child attends:

_____

_____

26. Do you participate in your language community? Please explain.

_____

_____

27. Other information you would like to share with your child's teacher:

_____

_____

APPENDIX 5.B

Language Fact Sheet

The following information about language can be shared with young children:
- Children can talk; adults can talk.
- Animals and babies can't.
- Animals communicate a limited number of messages.
- Apes and bonobo monkeys have been taught human sign language. Young children will find gorilla communication fascinating. See the website Koko Kid's Club for information about gorilla habits and abilities: http://www.koko.org/kidsclub/learn/10facts.html.
- Like people, languages belong to families.
- There are roughly 6,500 spoken languages in the world today. They are believed to have originated from one mother language.
- The most widely spoken language in the world is Mandarin.
- The Philippines has more than 1,000 regional dialects and two official languages.
- More than 1,000 different languages are spoken on the continent of Africa.
- Words that describe a particular cultural practice or idea may not translate precisely into another language.
- In many languages around the world, the word for "mother" begins with an M sound.
- The following body parts allow us to speak: tongue, lips, larynx or voice box, and vocal folds.
- To produce a phrase, about 100 muscles of the chest, neck, jaw, tongue, and lips must work together.
- Each spoken word or short phrase is accompanied by its own pattern of muscular movements.

- All the information necessary for speaking a phrase like "Good morning" is stored in the speech area of the brain.
- Early humans probably had a rudimentary speech system resembling animal communication.
- The first symbolic language emerged 2.5 million years ago, when early humans created tools.
- The brain has a "critical period," a time when it acquires speech.
- If language is not acquired at this time, the child will not acquire speech later on.

CHAPTER 6

ADOPTING LAP IN THE CLASSROOM

Our classrooms are now physically ready for LAP: the language policy is clearly displayed, the language centre is in place, charts showing classroom home languages are in full view, and the classroom set-up and background music reflect the home languages of the children.

In this chapter, we will turn our attention to five issues that are central to the adoption of LAP: transitioning immigrant children from home to classroom; introducing a new immigrant child; partnering with families; using home languages in the classroom; and language and literacy record keeping.

Immigrant Children's Home-Classroom Transition

Before we look at ways to help immigrant children make the move from home to the classroom, let's define *transition* as it applies to young immigrant children. The journey from the home to the classroom is far more than a short-term, language-learning event for the immigrant child who has no friends and does not speak the classroom language. It is an ongoing circumstance that affects the young child's personal, social, emotional, linguistic, and cognitive development directly. The effective transition of immigrant children should include bridging and sharing.[1] Namely, EC practitioners should take the time to understand immigrant children's home experiences, link these with classroom happenings, and partner with parents.

....

1 This definition of immigrant children's transition from home to classroom is adapted from earlier transition reports: Bohan-Baker and Little (2002), Kagan and Neuman (1998), Kraft-Sayre and Pianta (2000), and Zigler and Kagan (1982).

Five suggestions are provided to help you transition immigrant children. Activities that link children's home experiences to the classroom can be found in Chapter 7.

1. Involve the class as you welcome newcomers. In an age-appropriate way, discuss the following:
    (a) How does it feel to join a new group, have no friends, be away from home, or not understand or speak the classroom language?
    (b) How can we help? What can we do to make a new child feel welcome, comfortable, and happy?
2. Make a concrete plan to help a new child feel welcomed and comfortable by assigning specific tasks:
    (a) Find children and adults who speak the new arrival's home language.
    (b) Encourage the use of the child's home language.
    (c) Invite children to act as guides and take the new child on a classroom and school tour.
3. Encourage parents, grandparents, and other family members to do the following:
    (a) Spend time in the classroom when dropping off or picking up their children or grandchildren.
    (b) Use the home language as they interact with their children in the classroom.
    (c) Bring their children's favourite book or toy to the classroom.
    (d) Make name cards for their children in the home languages.
4. Call the home in the evening of the child's first day and tell the parents the following:
    (a) You are happy to have the child in your classroom.
    (b) There are children or adults in the school who speak the home language, or, if there are not, how you plan to work with them or with others outside of the school to ensure the child's comfort.
    (c) They are welcome in the classroom.
    (d) They are invited to participate in classroom activities.
5. Add the child's name and home language to the classroom language displays.[1]

....
1   See Chapter 7 for a list of classroom language displays.

Introducing and Welcoming a New Immigrant Child

When introducing a new child to the class, refer to her or his home experiences. Refer to the home language as something special and positive. The "Sample Introduction" provided in the text box can be adapted to children's ages and circumstances.

> **SAMPLE INTRODUCTION**
>
> This is Soo Hee.
>
> She is joining our class.
>
> Soo Hee has a new baby brother.
>
> Soo Hee speaks Korean.
>
> She comes from Korea.
>
> Korea is far away.
>
> Soo Hee travelled by plane to come to Toronto.
>
> Let's find Korea on our map of the world and on our globe.
>
> Who speaks Korean?
>
> Let's say HELLO and WELCOME to Soo Hee in English and French.
>
> How do we say HELLO and WELCOME in Korean?
>
> Let's add Soo Hee and her language to our language book and our language charts.
>
> This is Soo Hee's favourite book.
>
> It sure looks interesting.
>
> Let's ask her mom or dad to come and read it with us.

Partnering with Families

Parents and grandparents are your strongest allies in LAP. In fact, building meaningful relationships with families is key to the effective adoption of LAP. To open your doors to languages that, in many cases, you do not understand or speak and to link home and classroom experiences, you need parents and grandparents as partners. When EC practitioners partner with families, everyone

wins. Classrooms become multilingual environments, all children benefit, families feel connected and welcomed, home languages are promoted, and the bilingual goals of parents and EC practitioners come closer to being realized. Here are some of the benefits of partnering with families.

PARENTS AND GRANDPARENTS

- have a voice in the classroom life of their child or grandchild,
- become proactive in their child or grandchild's language learning,
- become valued educational partners,
- share their experiences and their language and literacy knowledge,
- bring home languages and literacies into the classroom,
- provide children with home language models,
- realize the bilingual hopes they have for their children, and
- discover different languages and cultures.

IMMIGRANT CHILDREN

- have language models,
- develop and showcase their home language and literacy skills,
- grow in linguistic awareness and understanding, and
- witness and experience various languages and literacies.

MONOLINGUAL CHILDREN

- witness and experience various languages and literacies,
- grow in linguistic awareness and understanding,
- develop an interest in learning a second language, and
- develop an interest in their heritage language.

EC PRACTITIONERS

- have support in their inclusive, multilingual teaching,
- learn about different languages and cultures, and
- link children's two language worlds.

Informing Families about LAP

The first step in gaining the support of families is to tell them about LAP. Using Appendix 6.A as a guide, prepare a letter that will inform families about the following: the benefits of a multilingual teaching approach, the promotion of bilingualism, bringing home languages and literacies into the classroom, and the importance of parental engagement.

The Language Committee

Using Appendix 6.B as a guide, invite families to join the "Language Committee," a parent group that will take on the following four tasks:

1. Participate in language-related classroom activities.
2. Translate classroom materials into home languages.
3. Provide resources (brochures, posters, books, CDs, DVDs) in home languages.
4. Post information about community events on the classroom news board.

In the next chapter, suggestions will be provided for family participation in language-related classroom activities.

The Language Thinking of Immigrant Parents

Understanding the language thinking of immigrant parents will allow the EC practitioner to identify their language goals, respond to their language concerns, and help link home and classroom experiences.

To understand how immigrant parents think about language, let's look at the findings of an early bilingualism study (Chumak-Horbatsch, 2008). The researcher asked one group of mothers and fathers of children enrolled in a Toronto childcare centre to respond to questions about their children's language learning. The children were

> "... we have to recognize that parents are invested in their emergent bilingual children's learning and want them to excel." *(García & Kleifgen, 2010, p. 101)*

between the ages of 1 year, 9 months and 3½ years at the time of the study. Even though the sample in this study is small, the reported views are typical of those held by parents who face language challenges in a new country. Parents wanted their children to achieve fluency in both the classroom and the home languages, but they were unsure about their role in teaching language and whether learning multiple languages might cause their children to become confused.

Bilingual Hopes of Immigrant Parents

The bilingual hopes reported by parents in the early bilingualism study are in line with the goals of LAP: parents want their children to walk in two language worlds, to maintain the home language, and to learn the classroom language. They strongly believe that knowing the home language is important for communication with immediate and extended family members and for their children's cultural membership and engagement. They also believe that learning the classroom language will lead to their children's school success and acceptance in the majority culture.

Language Concerns of Immigrant Parents

Along with their hopes for the bilingual future of their children, the mothers and fathers who participated in the early bilingualism study reported three language concerns:

- Parental role in children's home language learning: How can parents best fulfill the challenging role of ensuring fluency and literacy in the home language?
- Language parenting of mothers and fathers: What can be done to balance the language parenting of mothers and fathers?
- Bilingualism—advantages or confusion? Will exposure to two languages confuse or help children?

These three language concerns are briefly described below, and a workshop response is provided for each.

CONCERN #1: THE PARENTAL ROLE IN CHILDREN'S HOME LANGUAGE LEARNING

The mothers and fathers in the early bilingualism study reported that they have little control over their children's learning of the home language. They described the teaching of the home language as a challenging parental responsibility. They felt that EC practitioners cannot help because they do not speak the home languages. Yet mothers (but not fathers) reported that support and suggestions from EC practitioners for maintaining the home language would be most welcome.

Workshop: Yes You Can!

In this workshop, parents are reminded that they play a *pivotal* role in their children's home language learning. A three-part model, entitled "Believe-Commit-Provide (BCP)," illustrated in Figure 6.1, can be used as a discussion starter to help parents understand their role in their children's learning of the home language.

Believe: The first step in the BCP model encourages parents to believe that
- they play a central role in their children's learning of the home language,
- the home is the main context for home language learning and maintenance, and

- young children will grow into bilinguals if parents approach the home language with confidence.

Commit: The second step in the BCP model invites parents to commit to
- using the home language with children in the home;
- serving as home language models;
- adopting realistic, age-appropriate home language rules; and
- adapting home language rules as children grow and circumstances change.

Provide: The third step in the BCP model suggests that parents provide
- a home filled with rich and meaningful home language experiences;
- home language literacy activities, such as book sharing and letter writing; and
- intimate, informal, and spontaneous home language experiences.

FIGURE 6.1: Believe-Commit-Provide (BCP) Model

To reinforce the BCP model, the 14-minute DVD entitled *Your Home Language: Foundation for Success*[1] can be used to generate further discussion and encourage parents to share their language-parenting strategies. In addition to English and French, the DVD is available in Bengali, Punjabi, Russian, Somali, Farsi/Persian, Spanish, Gujarati, Tamil, Korean, Urdu, Mandarin, and Vietnamese.

CONCERN #2: LANGUAGE PARENTING OF MOTHERS AND FATHERS
The mothers who participated in the early bilingualism study were more committed to home languages than were their spouses. Maternal language parenting was focused on home languages while the fathers were more tolerant

....

1 *Your Home Language: Foundation for Success* is available from the Toronto District School Board. Contact curriculumdocs@tdsb.on.ca to purchase the DVD, or watch it online at http://www.tdsb.on.ca/_site/viewitem.asp?siteid=13&menuid=20006&pageid=17500.

and accepting of their children's learning of the classroom language. The mothers encouraged and expected their children to use home languages in the home, provided home language equivalents when the children used words in the classroom language, and read home language books regularly to their children. Unlike their spouses, the mothers were concerned and anxious about their children's increasing mixing of languages and loss of the home language. In contrast, the fathers were more focused on the learning of the classroom language and expressed pride in their children's hasty progress. They read more English-language books to their children than did mothers and directly taught English words and phrases to their children.

Workshop: Fathers Only
Planning a "Fathers Only" workshop can be challenging because many dads believe that concerns and issues related to children are the responsibility of the mothers. However, an invitation to discuss informally their language parenting and their children's dual language and literacy learning could bring fathers together for an evening of sharing.

The purpose of this workshop is twofold: to help fathers understand their role in children's home language and literacy learning and to encourage them to support their spouses in language parenting. The three suggestions that follow will help you organize a "Fathers Only" workshop.

1. List and discuss fathers' home language and literacy practices.
2. Explain the importance of spousal support in children's home language and literacy learning.
3. Use the BCP model to explain the role of both parents in children's home language learning.

CONCERN #3: BILINGUALISM—ADVANTAGES OR CONFUSION?
All the mothers and fathers who participated in the early bilingualism study reported advantages to knowing two languages. However, the mothers (but not the fathers) were worried about the possible negative effects of speaking the home language on the learning of the classroom language. Mothers and fathers also felt that exposure to two languages could cause difficulties later on when their children went to school.

Workshop: Bilingual Myths and Facts
The purpose of this workshop is to dispel some of the myths that parents reported about their children's dual language and literacy learning. A discussion

of bilingual myths and facts (see Table 6.1) will help clear up the confusion surrounding young children's dual language and literacy learning.

TABLE 6.1: Bilingual Myths and Facts

BILINGUAL MYTHS	BILINGUAL FACTS
STOP	**GO**
NOT TRUE!	**TRUE!**
• Young children acquire a second language with ease and require no support.	• Young children require a language-rich environment and meaningful interaction to acquire a second language.
• Learning two languages is confusing to children.	• Learning two languages is *not* confusing to young children.
• Using the home language will hinder progress in the classroom language.	• Using the home language will help the child make progress in the classroom language.
• Young children can only manage one language at a time.	• With sufficient exposure, support, and guidance, young children can manage two languages at the same time.
• A child who learns two languages will never be comfortable in either of them.	• A child who learns two languages will be enriched by two cultures.

The website http://www.ryerson.ca/mylanguage provides research-based information about bilingualism and the importance of maintaining home languages. The goal of the website is to help immigrant parents and EC practitioners understand children's dual language and literacy learning. The "Hold On" brochure, which explains the importance of maintaining children's home languages, is available in English, French, Mandarin, Polish, Romanian, Russian, Turkish, and Ukrainian. It is also available in PowerPoint format (in English). It can be used in workshops to help parents understand the nature and the advantages of bilingualism. Parents serving on the Language Committee can provide additional translations of the "Hold On" brochure.

In summary, families have an important role to play in LAP. Informing them about your inclusive classroom practice, encouraging them to bring their home languages and literacies into the classroom, and inviting them to join a parent language group will provide the support needed to implement LAP. Organizing workshops on topics of concern to immigrant parents can affect their language parenting positively.

Using Home Languages in the Classroom

EC practitioners who are speakers of heritage languages should not hesitate to use these languages in the classroom. Using home languages will provide an emotionally secure environment for newly arrived children who do not understand the classroom language, create a link between the home and the classroom, reinforce the importance of home languages, provide immigrant children with a home language model, and offer *all* children the opportunity to experience different languages.

CAREFUL LISTENING!

An EC practitioner reports that when she reads stories to her Mandarin-speaking preschoolers, their peers often join the group and appear fascinated as they listen to the sounds of a new language—especially when a familiar story is read.

Use home languages in the classroom

- reassure new arrivals who are anxious and fearful,
- communicate with parents whose proficiency in the classroom language is minimal,
- share home language books individually or in small groups, and
- conduct language-related activities.[1]

Language and Literacy Record Keeping

LAP requires EC practitioners to be linguistically vigilant and to take the time to observe and record children's language and literacy behaviours throughout the year. An effective way of doing this is to conduct "in-house" record keeping. Also known as "developmental evaluation," this form of record keeping is an ongoing, real-time, non-judgmental process that will identify key developmental moments and help you keep track of children's language and literacy growth and progress (see Patton, 2002 for more details). Before we look at suggestions for creating and using language and literacy records (L&L records), let's explore the benefits of this undertaking.

---

1 Language-related activities are presented in Chapter 7.

Benefits of Language and Literacy Records

L&L records are open, transparent documents that provide information about children's language and literacy development. Their many benefits far outweigh the time required to create and maintain them.

Sharing the L&L records with families will

- keep them informed about children's language and literacy skills, progress, and strengths;
- identify areas of concern;
- help sustain home-classroom partnerships; and
- encourage families to become more engaged in their children's language and literacy learning.

In cases where intervention is needed, L&L records will provide other professionals—for example, speech and language pathologists or medical practitioners—with information about children's language and literacy behaviours in the home and in the classroom.

It is important to talk to children about their language and literacy learning. Sharing selective information from L&L records with them will

- show them that their language learning is important;
- treat them as independent and unique language learners;
- validate their home language and literacy lives;
- make them proud owners of their home languages;
- help develop their metalinguistic skills, that is, their ability to reflect on and think and talk about language and literacy;
- provide the opportunity to evaluate their language and literacy progress;
- encourage the sharing of language and literacy experiences;
- acknowledge and celebrate achievements and progress; and
- encourage the setting of new language and literacy learning goals.

L&L records will also benefit the EC practitioner. Knowing how children use words, print, and books in the classroom will allow the EC practitioner to connect home and classroom language and literacy experiences and enable them to share information with families and children. The information contained in the L&L records will also provide a basis for program assessment and for the preparation of "L&L Report Cards," which document the language and literacy skills, challenges, strengths, preferences, and progress of each child. These report cards can be shared with parents.

How to Record

Ideally, recording should begin shortly after the start of the school year or at the time of registration. Given the busy pace of the classroom, it is important to plan and schedule your L&L record keeping.

The age of the children will determine the kind of observation and recording you will undertake. EC practitioners working in childcare centres with young children (aged 12–15 months who are not yet using words) will observe and record prelanguage behaviours. Those working with older children (toddlers, preschoolers, kindergarteners, and those in the primary grades) will pay attention to language use and developing literacy behaviours.

Select individual children for in-depth, half-day L&L observation. Prepare a monthly schedule to help keep tabs on which children are to be observed on which days, ensuring that each child is observed at least once during each month. This schedule will allow you to chart L&L progress, growth, change, developmental moments, and challenges.

What Are You Writing?

As you record L&L behaviours, a child may ask you what you are doing. It is both dishonest and poor pedagogy to respond with "Not much" or "Nothing." Such responses silence the curious child and downplay the purpose and meaning of a basic literacy skill. Here are some suggestions for answering children's "what" and "why" questions:

WHAT ARE YOU DOING?
I'm writing down
- what's happening here/at this table/in this corner.
- what this group/child is doing/saying.
- something important.
- what Joey is saying.
- the words Beverly is using.
- the languages these children are speaking.
- the way they are talking.

WHY?
I'm taking notes because
- this is important.
- I want to write down what I see and hear.
- the words are really interesting.
- I'd like to share this with others.
- I'd like to know if this activity/game is fun.
- I want to know if something is missing/if everything is OK.

What to Record

Preverbal Children

As you observe younger children, pay attention to and record prelanguage and preliteracy behaviours. The preverbal and preliteracy record (Appendix 6.C) includes a list of behaviours to note and record.

Older Children

With older children, L&L record keeping will be more complex. You will encounter different levels of classroom language proficiency. In the same way, children's home language abilities will range from single word use to full sentences. Also, some children will translanguage more than others. Literacy behaviours will also be quite different across children: some will have extensive and rich book-sharing experiences while others will be novices in their understanding of what books have to offer. As you observe and record, pay attention to L&L skills in both the classroom *and* the home languages. The listening and speaking record (Appendix 6.D) and the literacy skills record (Appendix 6.E) will help you in these tasks.

How Can I Record Languages I Don't Speak?

It is understandable for the EC practitioner to question the purpose of making notes, even general ones, about a language she or he does not know. However, there are personal and educational benefits for the EC practitioner in documenting children's home language and literacy behaviours:

- Helps develop an "ear for languages" so that one becomes skilled in identifying different languages.
- Increases knowledge and awareness of the languages of the world.
- Makes linguistic diversity come to life.
- Serves as a reminder that the EC practitioner is a learner.

If you observe children using their home language in the classroom, simply note this on the listening and speaking record (Appendix 6.D). For example, if you observe a child looking at a book and talking to herself in the home language, record the following:

Sitting alone, looking at book, using words in the HL (home language).

Another example: If you witness two children using the classroom language *and* their home language, make the following entry:

Using English and Mandarin with Li. Laughing, repeating Mandarin words, playing with words.

Staff who are speakers of home languages can help make more detailed recordings of home languages.

Summary

The stage is now set for LAP: new immigrant children are welcomed and included upon arrival, families are invited to join as classroom partners, home languages are heard in the classroom, and plans have been put in place to document children's language and literacy behaviours systematically.

The activities found in the next chapter are the exciting part of LAP—they will enrich the lives of the entire classroom community as they make languages and literacies come alive.

Key Points

1. For immigrant children, the transition from home to classroom is a long-term event that should be shared with families and closely linked to home experiences.
2. Involving the entire class in welcoming newcomers will ease their transition from home to the classroom.
3. Parents and grandparents are important partners in LAP.
4. The Language Committee is a parent group that takes on language-related tasks.
5. Understanding the language thinking of immigrant parents will help the EC practitioner identify their language goals, respond to their language concerns, and link children's home and classroom experiences.
6. Immigrant parents have bilingual hopes for their young children.
7. Immigrant parents have concerns about their children's dual language and literacy learning.
8. Organizing workshops on topics of concern to immigrant parents can affect their language parenting positively.
9. There are many benefits to using home languages in the classroom.
10. Language and literacy records are open, transparent documents that provide information about children's language and literacy development. Their many benefits far outweigh the time required to create and maintain them.

Group Activities

1. A New Arrival in the Classroom

Prepare a "Welcome List" that includes ways to make newly arrived children feel welcomed and comfortable. As you prepare your list, consider the following:

- Different ways of involving the class in transitioning new arrivals.
- Different ways of linking home and classroom experiences for newly arrived children.

2. Families as Partners

Bringing families into the classroom can be a challenge. Some parents are too busy to take an active part in the life of the classroom while others might feel unsure about what could be expected of them. For parents with limited proficiency in the classroom language, accepting an invitation to share their experiences may be awkward and uncomfortable.

In your group, discuss strategies that you currently use or could use to engage families.

APPENDIX 6.A

Sample Letter to Parents: Introducing Your Multilingual Classroom

Dear Parents and Guardians,

Welcome to our classroom! We are excited to begin our new school year.

The children in our classroom speak many different languages. At last count, we had speakers of the following nine languages: (list the languages).

Our teachers are also speakers of a number of languages: Miss Pearl speaks Mandarin, Miss Luiska speaks Polish, and Mr. Tahir is a speaker of Urdu.

Our classroom door is open to all languages. Knowing how important languages are, we support and promote bilingualism.

Throughout the year, we will help all children learn and grow in the classroom language. We will also support families as they help their children develop in their home languages. In our lessons and activities, we will include home languages. We will talk about different ways of speaking, writing, singing, and living. We invite you to join our discussions, projects, and activities. Come and share your languages and your talents with us.

Please check our classroom news board regularly. On it, you will find a monthly calendar of planned activities, with dates, times, and a sign-up sheet.

We look forward to seeing you in our classroom.

Sincerely,

APPENDIX 6.B

....

Sample Letter of Invitation: Language Committee

....

Dear Parents and Guardians,

We invite you to join the Language Committee, a parent group that will bring home languages into the classroom. In addition to English, we have nine languages represented in our classroom: (list languages here). It is important that we have a parent-representative from each home language.

The Language Committee will take on the following tasks:

- participate in language-related classroom activities,
- translate classroom materials,
- provide resources and materials in the home language, and
- post information about community events on the classroom news board.

Our first meeting will be held on (insert date) at (insert time), in (insert location).

We look forward to seeing you.

Sincerely,

APPENDIX 6.C

Preverbal and Preliteracy Record

PREVERBAL AND PRELITERACY BEHAVIOURS

CHILD'S NAME: _____ **AGE:** ____ **DATE:** _____

PRELITERACY BEHAVIOURS
- Enjoys looking at books, listening to simple stories, singing.
- Responds to pictures when asked: "Where's the cat? Show me the cat."
- Displays reading-like behaviour: holds book upright, turns pages, looks at and points to words.
- Recognizes own name in print.
- Enjoys making marks on paper.

DATE   **OBSERVED BEHAVIOURS**

_____   _____

_____   _____

APPENDIX 6.D

Listening and Speaking Record

LISTENING AND SPEAKING BEHAVIOURS

CHILD'S NAME: _____ **AGE:** ____ **DATE:** _____

LISTENING
- Listens attentively.
- Follows instructions and directions.
- Aware of language differences.

SPEAKING
- Social conventions of talking (turn taking, interrupting, tone of voice, use of gestures).

- Speaking in a group.
- Responding to/asking questions.
- Requesting/negating.
- Word knowledge/use.
- Telling/retelling stories.
- Using the home language.
- Translanguaging.
- Language play.
- Private speech.

DATE   **OBSERVED BEHAVIOURS**

_____   _____

_____   _____

APPENDIX 6.E

....

Literacy Skills Record

....

LITERACY BEHAVIOURS

CHILD'S NAME: _____   **AGE:** ____   **DATE:** _____

READING SKILLS
- Chooses books during self-selected activities.
- Understands that print carries meaning.
- Uses picture cues when talking about a book.
- Shows understanding of stories by connecting them to own experiences.
- Talks about favourite stories.
- Tells a story from pictures.
- Tells stories in sequence.
- Invents stories.
- Understands the direction of print.
- Recognizes letters, characters.
- Knows several words by sight.
- Recognizes nonsense in stories.
- Recalls main idea and details.
- Predicts what will happen next.
- Enjoys reading in the home language.
- Familiar with dual language books.
- Aware of language differences in books.

WRITING SKILLS
- Chooses crayon and paper during self-selected activities.
- Understands relationship between letter and sound
- Recognizes own name in print.
- Responds to/aware of signs in the classroom.
- Attempts to write own name in classroom/home language.
- Uses writing models.

MEDIA LITERACY
Shows an understanding of images and messages in various media forms:
- visual,
- spoken,
- acoustic,
- written, and electronic.

DATE   **OBSERVED BEHAVIOURS**

_____   _____

_____   _____

PART III

Implementing LAP Activities

"That's my flag! Vietnam. What's yours?"

CHAPTER 7

LAP ACTIVITIES

Your classroom is now set up as a multilingual, multi-literate environment. You have a new classroom language centre, and your classroom language policy is in place. You have addressed immigrant parents' language concerns and have ensured that EC practitioners use their language resources effectively in the classroom. Now comes the exciting and creative part—implementing LAP activities with the children and families!

> "A meaningful and rigorous education for emergent bilinguals will always use the home language as much as possible." (García & Kleifgen, 2010, p. 59)

What Are LAP Activities?

LAP activities cover a wide range of topics and subject areas. They are conducted in the classroom language and include a home language component. In some cases, LAP activities are conducted in home languages by parents, grandparents, or older children. With younger children (infants and toddlers) who are in the very early stages of language and literacy development in both the home and classroom languages, LAP activities will be simple and will be adult initiated and directed. For older children (preschoolers, kindergarteners, and primary graders) who are more proficient language users and, in most cases, have some literacy experiences, LAP activities will be more varied and comprehensive. When older children understand that their home languages have a place in the classroom and that their ideas and contributions are important, they will participate more fully in LAP activities, require less adult direction, and make these activities their own.

Why Use LAP Activities?

Participation in LAP activities will help *all* children engage in personal and group identity construction and negotiation. Exposure to different languages will help them work through questions such as "Who am I?" and "Who are you?" and "Who are we?" It will also help them understand that languages link speakers to specific behaviours and groups. For example, immigrant children will realize that, in addition to belonging to home language and cultural groups, they are members of the classroom language community. They will see that their language worlds need not be separate—that there is a place for all languages in the classroom. These experiences will encourage them to use and develop their home languages and to learn the classroom language. In classrooms where a variety of languages are included and explored, monolingual children will affirm their language identities, discover new worlds, and perhaps express an interest in learning a new language.

When children participate in LAP activities, they will discover how other people talk, live, sing, eat, pray, cook, and count. These activities will help develop important science and math skills and promote an understanding of local and global community life.

I KNOW FRENCH!

Five-year-old Meaghan, a monolingual English speaker, attends a morning French immersion program. When she arrives in her English-language childcare centre in the afternoon, she is very excited about French words. She points to objects in the classroom and asks me to supply the French word. Having some proficiency in French, I can play this game to a point. However, when I don't know a word, Meaghan proudly names the object in French. As I praise her knowledge of French, she turns to her friend and says, "I speak French."

LAP activities will enrich and enhance language arts curriculum

LAP activities will help *all* children develop skills in four areas of the classroom language: oral communication, reading, writing, and media literacy.[1] In Canada, specific skills in these four broad areas or "strands" can be found in

---

1 Media literacy refers to the ability to access, analyze, evaluate, and create messages that communicate information and ideas in various media forms—print, oral, visual, or electronic—using words, graphics, sounds, or images.

the English and French language arts school curricula, which are developed for each educational level, from kindergarten to high school.[1]

Finally, including French and English in LAP activities with young children will serve as a stepping stone for their later French or English instruction.

How to Use LAP Activities

The successful implementation of LAP activities requires careful preparation, planning, and scheduling. The EC practitioner is encouraged to consult the references included throughout this chapter for important background information and resources.

> "Although a monolingual teacher cannot actually 'teach' students' native languages, that teacher can create a multi-literate community." *(Schwarzer, Haywood, & Lorenzen, 2003, p. 455)*

The activities are presented in broad terms. It is the task of the EC practitioner to adapt each activity to the specific needs of the children and to plan how best to engage the children and families.

EC practitioners are *promoters*—and not teachers—of home languages. Although the home language component of the LAP activities validates and supports home languages and provides some opportunity for continued learning, the main responsibility for the development of oral communication, reading, writing, and media literacy skills in home languages remains in the home.

The four suggestions that follow will help the EC practitioner implement LAP activities.

Take the time to talk with the children as you introduce a LAP activity.
- This will allow you to gauge their level of understanding, their previous experiences, and their interests. With this information, you will be able to determine how best to engage them.

Engage and involve children and their families in planning and implementing LAP activities.
- For example, children can suggest and help prepare the place where the sign-in book will be displayed (see Theme 1, Activity 1.1). They can decorate the covers. Older children can be given the task of

---

1 In Canada, language arts curriculum guidelines, like those for other subject areas, are prepared and prescribed by provincial education ministries. They define English and French language learning, outline English and French language knowledge and the specific skills children are expected to develop at each grade level, and serve as a provincial standard for all educators.

printing the date on each page. Parents can write their children's names in their home languages.

Take your cues from children and families.
- Look for areas of interest, issues, challenges, highlights, and successes. These will help guide how an activity unfolds and determine potential extensions.

Extend the LAP activities.
- After implementing the activities as described in this chapter, don't be afraid to think outside the box and make them your own. Encourage children and families to think of ways to extend the activities by changing the participants, the context, and materials.

The LAP activities found in this chapter come from several sources. Most were developed as a result of my numerous classroom visits and direct interactions with children, their families, and EC practitioners. Others are extensions and expansions of practices found in the reviewed publications (see Chapter 3). All LAP activities were reviewed by EC practitioners for suitability and appropriateness.

Organization of LAP Activities

The LAP activities are organized into five themes:

- THEME 1: Charting Home Languages
- THEME 2: Using Home Languages in the Classroom
- THEME 3: Linking the Home and Classroom
- THEME 4: Bringing the Outside World into the Classroom
- THEME 5: Sharing Books and Newspapers with Children

The five themes are interrelated. This means that many of the activities could easily fit into more than one theme. For example, the bilingual name card activity (Theme 1: Charting Home Languages, Activity 1.6) includes reading children's names in home languages, and could also be included in Theme 2: Using Home Languages in the Classroom. The tips included with most LAP activities provide the EC practitioner with implementation and follow-up suggestions. A complete list of all LAP activities by theme can be found in Appendix 7.A.

Table 7.1 shows the language configuration of a sample kindergarten classroom with 17 children and 2 EC practitioners. A total of six languages are spoken in the homes of the children and the practitioners. This kindergarten classroom will be used throughout the chapter to illustrate the LAP activities.

TABLE 7.1: Home Languages of a Sample Kindergarten Class

LANGUAGE	NUMBER OF SPEAKERS	SPEAKERS
English	3	Miss Ross, Joshua, Elizabeth
Mandarin	4	Huan, Lin, Shan, Miss Pearl
Arabic	3	Amira, Baraka, Akbar
Urdu	3	Sabirah, Johara, Tahir
Polish	1	Agnieczka
Farsi	5	Ali, Sadri, Karim, Azin, Navid

THEME 1: Charting Home Languages

In the nine activities included in the first theme, home languages are recorded, discussed, printed, read, sorted, compared, and graphed. These activities are intended mostly for older children. However, with the help of adults or older children (in multi-age settings, for example), many of these activities can be adapted for use with younger children.

Activity 1.1: The Sign-In Book

Using a large sketchbook (11½" x 14"), prepare a monthly sign-in book. The cover will include the name of the month, and the full date will appear at the top of each page. Invite the children to print their names in the book when they arrive in the morning. (See Photo 7.1 for a sample page from a kindergarten sign-in book.)

PHOTO 7.1: Page from a Kindergarten Sign-In Book

Tips

- Encourage parents to help younger children sign in and add their names in their home languages.
- The sign-in book can serve as a monthly attendance sheet.
- It can be shared with parents

to show them how their child's name-making skills are evolving.

- Older children can be encouraged to include their first and last names in both the classroom language and in their home languages.
- Place the sign-in book on a low table beside the entrance. Add a cup full of coloured markers, crayons, pastels, or fine-tipped pens to make signing in more inviting.

THAT'S MY NAME!

One morning, five-year-old Soon Bok carefully prints her name in Korean and in English in the classroom sign-in book. Later that same day, she returns to the sign-in book with her classmate Joel, a monolingual speaker of English. Soon Bok points to her name and proudly announces, "That's my name. That's my name in English. And that's my name in Korean, you know. I'm Korean, and that's how I make my name in Korean."

Activity 1.2: The Colours of Our Home Languages

Working with the children, assign a colour for each home language. Using coloured dot stickers, make a chart showing the different colours and the names of the languages. Display the language chart in the language centre. For a sample home language chart, see the text box entitled "Our Home Languages."

OUR HOME LANGUAGES

(red dot) Arabic	(green dot) Mandarin
(orange dot) English	(pink dot) Polish
(yellow dot) Farsi	(purple dot) Urdu
(blue dot) French	

Tips

- Some children will have more than one home language. Invite parents to add each language spoken in their household using the name and script of that language.
- Be sure to have a supply of coloured stickers on hand—they will be used in other activities.
- Don't forget to add French and English to the home languages list.
- Keep the language chart updated as new children arrive in your classroom.

Activity 1.3: The Colour of My Home Language

The leader of this simple game can be the EC practitioner, a family member, or a child. With the "Our Home Languages" chart in full view, the leader calls out, points to, or displays one of the language colours. In response, children who speak that language raise their hands. For example, when "green" is called out or pointed to, children who speak Mandarin at home raise their hands, or when an orange circle is held up, children who speak English at home raise their hands.

Tips

- When the French (or English) colour is displayed, children can be reminded that this is one of the official languages of Canada.
- Invite the French or English teacher (or a speaker of French or English) to visit the classroom to tell the children about Canada's two languages.

Activity 1.4: Our Home Language Book

The home language book is a classroom album of names and home languages created by the children. Prepare this book using large (11½" x 14") blank pages, allowing one page for each home language. Invite the children to use the assigned home language colours to write their names on the appropriate page or pages.

FIGURE 7.1: Sample Home Language Book

Tips

- Parents can help children write their names in their home languages.
- Invite the children to decorate the book with pictures, flags, and photos.
- Keep the home languages book updated as new children arrive in your classroom.
- Extend the project to the whole school or childcare centre by engaging the children from different classrooms to prepare a joint home languages book.
- Encourage children to "read" the home language book: for example, "Elizabeth, Joshua, and Miss Ross speak English at home. Baraka, Akbar, and Amira speak Arabic at home."

Activity 1.5: Our Home Language Tree

With the help of the children, prepare a construction paper tree trunk and enough blank leaves for all of the classroom home languages. Invite the children to use the assigned language colours to print their names in the classroom and home languages on the leaves that correspond to their home languages. Display the home language tree in the language centre.

PHOTO 7.2: Sample Home Language Tree

Tips

- Invite the children to add photos, drawings, greetings, and flags to the leaves. See the examples in Figure 7.2.
- Make this a family classroom activity by inviting the parents to help the children print their names in home languages.

FIGURE 7.2: Home Language Tree Displays

Activity 1.6: Bilingual Name Cards

Invite parents of younger children to print their child's name in the home languages on the back of classroom name cards. Older children can do this on their own. The example below shows the child's name in English and, on the reverse side, in Arabic.

FIGURE 7.3: Sample Bilingual (English-Arabic) Name Card

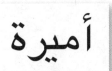

أميرة   Amira

Tips

- Invite the children to add the sticker of their language colour to their name cards.
- Encourage the children to refer to the bilingual name cards when they sign their artwork.

Activity 1.7: Home Language Graphs

Using the information found in your classroom home language chart (see "Our Home Languages" text box, Activity 1.2), work with the children to develop different graphs: bar graphs, line graphs, and pie charts. The developmental level of the children will be your guide as to the kinds of graphs you prepare. Display the home languages graphs in the language centre.

Tips

The following can be charted or graphed:

- language names in alphabetical order;
- languages in order, from lowest number of speakers in the classroom to highest number of speakers;
- languages in order, from highest number of speakers in the classroom to lowest number of speakers;
- languages that use letters;
- languages that use characters; and
- languages in order, from highest to lowest or lowest to highest number of letters or characters;
- computers can help children generate many different sorts of charts and graphs of home languages.

Activity 1.8: Sorting Classroom Books by Language

Displaying books in home languages and books with bilingual texts (dual language books) is a common practice in classrooms with immigrant children. However, these books too often remain on the bookshelf for long periods of time and go unnoticed by the children. Engaging the children in sorting classroom books by language can help make these books more visible and accessible.

Working with the children, categorize all classroom books by language. Make signs for the shelves or boxes where the books are stored. At the end of the day or week, conduct a "book check" with the children to ensure that the books are in the correct places.

FIGURE 7.4: Sample Book Sorting Signs

English (or French) Books	Dual Language Books	Home Language Books

Activity 1.9: Country, Flag, and Language Chart

Visit the following website with the children: http://www.flags.net/mainindex.htm. Invite each child to locate and download the flag of his or her country of origin. Using these flags as models, invite the children to draw (or paint) their flags on sheets of white paper (18" x 12"). Using the language colour codes, invite the children to prepare a country-flag-language chart (see example in Figure 7.5). Encourage the children to print their names in the appropriate columns using the language colours of the class. Display the chart in the language centre.

"Here's my flag."

FIGURE 7.5: Sample Chart of Countries, Flags, and Languages

Country	Canada	Iran	Pakistan	Poland	China	Egypt
Flag						
Language	English	Farsi	Urdu	Polish	Mandarin	Arabic
Speakers	Miss Ross	Ali	Sabirah	Agnieczka	Huan	Amira
	Joshua	Sadri	Johara		Lin	Baraka
	Elizabeth	Karim	Tahir		Shan	Akbar
		Azin			Miss Pearl	
		Navid				

Tips

- In addition to downloading flags, write a letter asking parents to send "real" flags to the classroom.
- You may encounter families with two countries and flags. For example, the mother's country of origin may be different from the father's. Include both flags on the chart.
- Encourage the children to add the following information to extend the countries, flags, and languages chart:
  - National flower or tree of each country, e.g., the maple leaf for Canada (see http://www.theflowerexpert.com/content/aboutflowers/national-flowers).

- National bird, e.g., the loon for Canada (see http://www. camacdonald.com/birding/CountryIndex.htm).
- Number of colours in the flag.
- National sport, e.g., hockey or lacrosse for Canada.
- Use a map of the world and a globe to locate and mark all of the countries listed on the chart.
- Make a graph called "Flag Colours" and list the colours of each flag. Which flag has the most colours? Which flags have the same colours? What do the symbols on the flags represent?
- Invite parents to
  - provide the word for "flag" in each of the home languages,
  - explain the flag colours and symbols of their countries of origin,
  - provide additional information about their countries and
  - extend this activity to postage stamps from different countries.

FOLLOW-UP AT HOME

Following the country, flag, and language activity, a kindergarten child made the above picture at home and brought it to school to show his teacher. He described the four flags as "the flags of my friends."

Theme 2: Using Home Languages in the Classroom

The activities in Theme 2 include a significant home language component, which will require children, families, and EC practitioners to contribute home language words, phrases, greetings, songs, and chants.

Activity 2.1: Singing in Home Languages

Home languages can be added to everyday classroom singing (good morning songs, weather songs, and tidy up and farewell songs). You can also use home languages during the chanting of finger plays and poems.

To get started, you can invite parents to translate songs and poems and teach simple songs and poems to the children. The focus is on enjoyment and inclusion not on performance-oriented learning.

For more information on the strategies adopted in this multilingual classroom, see Schwarzer, Haywood, and Lorenzen (2003).

Another option is to use well-known songs that have become international, such as *Old MacDonald / La Ferme à Maturin / Nella Vecchia Fattoria*. For example, you could sing *Frère Jacques* in French and then in English. The melody is simple, and the words are repeated and easy to learn. Invite the French (or

> ## MULTILINGUAL SINGING IN THE CLASSROOM!
>
> An example of singing in home languages comes from a multilingual kindergarten classroom in Texas where, in addition to English, children spoke Korean, Chinese, Spanish, and Turkish in the home. Parents were asked to translate Itsy Bitsy Spider, a song that was part of the classroom's "creepy crawlies" theme. To help with pronunciation, the EC practitioner prepared a chart showing the words written out phonetically in English. The children were then grouped according to their home languages, with a parent leader or other speaker of the home language in each group. After learning the song in their home language, the children switched groups and learned the song in a new language. This activity proved to be exciting, and the EC practitioners reported that children enjoyed learning a familiar song in a new language.

English) language teacher to translate, sing along, and help with pronunciation. Invite parents to translate the words and sing *Frère Jacques* in home languages.

FRENCH	ENGLISH	POLISH
Frère Jacques	*Brother John*	*Bracie Janie*
Frère Jacques,	Are you sleeping?	Bracie Janie,
Frère Jacques,	Are you sleeping?	Bracie Janie,
Dormez-vous?	Brother John?	Pora wstać,
Dormez-vous?	Brother John?	Pora wstać,
Sonnez les matines.	Morning bells are ringing.	Wszystkie dzwony biją,

FRENCH	ENGLISH	POLISH
Sonnez les matines.	Morning bells are ringing.	Wszystkie dzwony biją,
Din, dan, don.	Ding, dong, ding.	Bim, bam, bom,
Din, dan, don.	Ding, dong, ding.	Bim, bam, bom.

Tips

- For translations of *Frère Jacques* see *Wikipedia*: http://en.wikipedia.org/wiki/Translations_of_Frère_Jacques
- Listen and sing along to YouTube clips of *Frère Jacques* in English and in French with the children:
- http://www.youtube.com/watch?v=XHX5k0NCdj4&feature=related (English)
- http://www.youtube.com/watch?v=Ds_plkgWQPg&feature=related (French)
- http://www.youtube.com/watch?v=_S5PvD9rP2g&feature=related (English and French)
- The *Mama Lisa's World* website (http://www.mamalisa.com) focuses on international music and culture and provides songs and nursery rhymes from around the world.

SINGING IN MANDARIN—MY WAY!

In the toddler room, I notice that Meilin is happily singing Twinkle, Twinkle Little Star to herself as she paints. "Can you sing Twinkle, Twinkle Little Star in Mandarin?" I ask her. She looks at me, smiles, and, keeping the song's melody and tempo, she loudly sings,

"Mandarin, Mandarin."

Activity 2.2: How Do You Say "Music" in Your Language?

Invite parents and children to provide translations of the word "music" in their home languages. Discuss the similarities across languages: e.g., English (*music*), French (*la musique*), and Polish (*muzyka*). Using as a guide the text box entitled "Music in Our Languages," prepare a chart with the word "music" translated into the classroom languages and written in the assigned home language colours.

Tips

- Invite the children to audio record their translations of the word "music." As you play back this recording, their task is to identify the language and the speaker.
- With the children, translate other music-related words, such as "choir," "piano," and "tone," into home languages.

> **Music in Our Languages**
>
> English   music
> French   la musique
> Mandarin   音乐
> Polish   muzyka

Activity 2.3: Morning Puzzler

Every morning, write a puzzler (riddle or hidden message) on the chart stand in the language centre. The children's task is to work together to solve the puzzler. The puzzler can be related to the lives and interests of the children, to classroom themes, or to school and community events. Morning puzzlers can include the identification or definition of words, numbers, symbols, pictures, and phrases written in the languages represented in the classroom. Once the children have had time to solve the morning puzzler on their own, discuss the solution as a group.

Tips

The morning puzzler could include the following:

- "Happy Birthday" printed in home languages and the classroom language (see http://www.shabbir.com/romance/bday.html).
- Family events: new baby brother or sister, wedding, travel.
- Classroom or school events: concerts, bake sales, exhibits, visitors
- Words, phrases, numbers that count down to special days, events, or holidays.
- A word list related to the theme under discussion.
- A classroom rule.
- A photo that portrays a strong emotion (happiness, pain, fear, sadness).
- Numbers and words for 1 to 10 in the classroom and home languages.
- Shapes or colours and their names in the classroom and home languages.
- Highlights of stories read.
- Newspaper or advertisement clips (in the classroom and home languages).

Activity 2.4: Calendar Time

There are a number of ways that home languages can be added to daily calendar time. Ask children to provide translations of calendar-related words such as days of the week, numbers, weather words, and colours. For example, you might ask, "Abkar, how do you say 'sunny' in Arabic?" or "Navid, what's the word for 'five' in your language?"

Tip

- Avoid putting children on the spot. Initially, they may be hesitant to contribute. However, when they see that their responses are valued, they will happily and proudly respond.

Activity 2.5: Calendars from Home

Ask children to bring calendars from home. Display these in the language centre, and colour code them.

Tip

- Invite parents to explain the main features of the calendars: name of language, writing system, direction of print, meaning and significance of pictures or symbols, and special days.

PRONOUNCING WORDS WITH UNFAMILIAR SOUNDS

Together with the children, attempt the pronunciation of words in different languages. As you do so, consult home language speakers by asking,

"Did we say that the right way?"

"Did we pronounce it correctly?"

"Let's try it again."

The novel and unfamiliar speech sounds will require several repetitions.

Dispel negative comments, such as "That's so stupid" or "That sounds silly," by emphasizing language differences and the unique language skills of individual children.

Activity 2.6: I Love Different Languages—Do You?

Using a tape recorder, record each child saying, "I love different languages—do you?" in her or his home language. As the tape is played back, the children try to identify two things: the language and the child's voice: "That was Arabic;

it's Baraka!" Once they are able to identify all of the classroom languages, add French (or English) to the recordings: *J'adore les langues différentes—et toi?* or "I love different languages—do you?"

Tip

- Related language activities, posters, and stickers can be found at http://www.whystudylanguages.ac.uk/ks3/love.

Activity 2.7: Language Ball

As a soft, medium-sized ball is passed around the circle, children provide translations of familiar words and simple phrases. For example, Miss Pearl, the EC practitioner in our sample kindergarten class, who speaks Mandarin, starts the game by holding the language ball and calling out "chair" and then *yizi*, which is Mandarin for "chair." She then passes the ball to Agnieczka, who is sitting beside her. Agnieczka says *krzesło* (Polish for "chair") and passes the ball to her neighbour. When every child has responded, Miss Pearl calls out a new word. Called out words can be numbers, shapes, colours, names of foods, or greetings. Once the children become familiar with the procedure, they can lead the game.

Tips

- This game can be played at a simple or more advanced level, in pairs or in a small group.
- Another variation is to have children who are sitting in a circle pass the language ball around as music plays. When the music stops, the child holding the ball says a selected word, phrase, or greeting in his or her home language.

Word Learning Activities: Introduction

A large oral vocabulary better prepares young children for learning to read and write than any other "readiness" exercises. The more words children know, the better they will understand themselves and their world and the easier it will be for them to formulate and express their thoughts. Word knowledge is one of the basic building blocks of language and literacy acquisition. In the preschool years, it is a strong predictor of later literacy skills, is closely associated with reading achievement, and can lead to better academic skills and school success.

But what about immigrant children's word knowledge in the home language and in the classroom language? Research on the relationship between young children's word knowledge and literacy development found the following.

- Word knowledge in the home language is related to learning the classroom language.

- Transfer of word knowledge occurs across languages.
- Literacy experiences in the child's first language will contribute to literacy development in the classroom language.[1]

Activity 2.8: "What Do You See?"

Using picture books with brightly coloured illustrations (colours, shapes, food, clothing, body parts, numbers, toys, and furniture), the child or adult points to each object and asks, "What do you see?" This activity is particularly appropriate for use with infants and toddlers, as it helps to build their vocabulary in the classroom language.

Tips

- Encourage parents to play this word game at home to build children's home language vocabularies.
- You can play this sort of game without even asking questions. (See the text box "Animal Names" for a description.)

ANIMAL NAMES

Four-year-old Deshi arrived from China on Friday and came to the childcare centre on Monday. On his third day, I saw him sitting by himself in the block centre, playing with animal figures. I sat down beside him and picked up a pig. I am a monolingual speaker of English who learned some animal names in Mandarin from a former co-worker. I held up the pig, looked at Deshi, and said zhu. Deshi looked at me, smiled, and nodded. I picked up a horse and said ma. Deshi nodded again, his smile getting brighter. Then, I picked up a lion. I didn't know the word for lion in Mandarin, so I looked at him and raised my eyebrows. Deshi took the lion from me, pointed to it, and slowly and clearly said shi zi. I repeated the word, and Deshi nodded. He then picked up a goat, slowly said yang, and waited for my repetition. We continued our game for almost 15 minutes. The next day, after we repeated our "Name the Animal" game, I showed Deshi this YouTube clip, which identifies different animals and shows how their names are represented using Chinese characters:
http://www.youtube.com/watch?v=VdOelTKmN1E

---

[1] For more information on the relationship between children's vocabulary and literacy skills, see Snow, Burns, and Griffin (1998) and Quiroz, Snow, and Zhao (2010).

Activity 2.9: Word Cards

Prepare index cards (5" x 8") with the following: greeting words, days of the week, months of the year, numbers, number words, pictures of common objects, and words related to classroom themes. Clipart websites, many of which are free, include a rich collection of pictures and symbols. Laminate the cards and store them in a sturdy "word box." For sample cards, see Figure 7.6.

FIGURE 7.6: Sample Word Cards

Following a demonstration by the EC practitioner, a child or a parent can lead this activity. The leader selects and holds up one of the cards from the word box, for example, the picture of a hand (see Figure 7.6). The children call out "hand" in the classroom language. The leader goes down the languages listed on the home languages chart (see Table 7.1) and asks the children to complete the following sentence:

The word for "hand" in Mandarin/Arabic/Urdu/etc. is _____.

Children who are speakers of the selected languages call out the translation for the word "hand."

Tips

- Encourage parents to play this word game in the home with their children.
- If children do not respond or say "I forget" or "I don't know," suggest that they consult their parents and report back the next day.

IT'S A SEVIVON!

Joshua is a three-year-old preschooler who, in addition to English, is learning some Hebrew at home. He attends a Toronto childcare centre where the language of program delivery is English. One morning Joshua arrives holding a small top-like object in his hand and loudly announces, "It's a sevivon!"

The mother explains that "sevivon" is the Hebrew word for dreidel (a Yiddish word), a spinning top used in games played by children and adults at Hanukkah.

(continues on next page)

A short while later, I go over to Joshua and ask, "What's the Hebrew word for dreidel?" He responds by repeating the word "sevivon" several times. When I repeat the word and mispronounce it, Joshua bursts out laughing. Determined to follow up on this incident, I use my iPhone and find all the information I need about the word "sevivon": the English and Hebrew script, definition, and pronunciation. I practice a few times and then come to Joshua with my accurate pronunciation. He is so happy that he starts dancing. Later in the day, I go to the art table with him and print the word "sevivon" in English and Hebrew. Joshua adds a picture and takes the card home.

Shortly after this incident, Joshua regularly brings cards from home with Hebrew words and numbers printed on them. To the delight of his parents, he practices counting in Hebrew and recognizes some of the words from his cards.

Activity 2.10: Hello–Goodbye Chart

With the help of parents, make a "Hello–Goodbye" chart that includes the languages represented in the classroom. Be sure to include French and English. Display the chart beside the door. As children arrive, greet them, or, as they leave, bid each farewell in his or her home language, encouraging all the children to respond in their home languages.

Tips

- For translations of "hello" and "goodbye," consult these websites:
  - http://users.elite.net/runner/jennifers/Greetings C.htm
  - http://users.elite.net/runner/jennifers/goodbye.htm
- Read this multi-language greeting book as a follow-up: Roche, D. (1999). *Can you greet the whole wide world? 12 common phrases in 12 different languages.* Boston: Houghton Mifflin.

Activity 2.11: Happy Birthday Chart

Working with the children, prepare a "Happy Birthday" chart that includes all the home languages represented in the classroom.

Tips

- The following website lists birthday greetings in various languages: http://www.freelang.net/expressions/birthday.php.
- Ask parents to teach the children birthday songs in their home languages.

- When celebrating or marking a birthday, sing "Happy Birthday" in the classroom language and also in the home language of the child celebrating his or her birthday.

Activity 2.12: Bilingual Greeting Cards

Have blank cards, pens, stickers, sparkles, markers, and doilies available for children to create bilingual or trilingual (English, French, home language) greeting cards for family members and friends. Encourage the children to create cards for birthdays, Mother's Day, Father's Day, Christmas, Chinese New Year, Thanksgiving, Diwali, Ramadan, Hanukah, and other special days.

In this photo, a five-year-old child adds a Polish greeting to a Christmas card for his parents.

Activity 2.13: Newspaper Letter and Word Hunt

Ask the children to search for letters and words in newspaper pages. The following can be highlighted, circled, or cut out: first letters (e.g., m, q, p, a), word endings (e.g., -ed -ly, -tion), small words (e.g., a, the, I, me, if, or, on, in, it), and longer words (e.g., today, open, maybe, was). Print the instructions on small index cards (3" x 5") that are kept in a box labelled "Newspaper Search." See Figure 7.7 for sample instruction cards.

FIGURE 7.7: Sample Instruction Cards

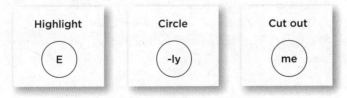

Once the task has been completed, ask the children to count and record the number of times specific letters, syllables, or words were found. Discuss the use of common and less common letters, syllables, and words.

Tip

■ This letter and word search can be extended to newspaper pages in home languages. Parents can prepare the instruction cards with letters, words, or characters that children will search, mark, and count and record.

Activity 2.14: Our Alphabets and Writing Systems

Using http://www.omniglot.com/, prepare a chart showing the different writing systems of the languages represented in the classroom. For example, in our sample six-language kindergarten, there are three different writing systems (Roman, Arabic, and Chinese), each with different numbers of letters or characters and a specific direction of writing (see Table 7.2). Display the chart in the language centre, and discuss the different writing systems with children. Explain that the systems have both similarities and differences. The developmental level of the children will be your guide when you prepare and discuss the writing systems chart.

TABLE 7.2: Sample Chart of Alphabets and Writing Systems

LANGUAGE	WRITING SYSTEM	NUMBER OF LETTERS / CHARACTERS	WRITING DIRECTION
English	Roman	26	L-R top to bottom
French	Roman	26	L-R top to bottom
Polish	Roman	36	L-R top to bottom
Urdu	Arabic	28	R-L top to bottom
Farsi	Arabic	32	R-L top to bottom
Arabic	Arabic	28	R-L top to bottom
Mandarin	Chinese	3,500 (basic)	R-L top to bottom

Tips

■ Encourage children to create dual language books showing the writing systems of their home languages and the classroom language.

■ Older children can prepare a short class presentation and share facts about the writing system of their home languages.

■ See Appendix 7.B for a list of picture books about different writing systems.

Activity 2.15: Numbers in Home Languages

Go to http://www.marijn.org/everything-is-4/counting-0-to-100 and familiarize yourself with the number systems of the languages represented in the
classroom. Together with the children, prepare a number chart showing the
language, numbers, and number words for each language. Table 7.3 shows the
number systems for English, Urdu, and Mandarin. The number words appear
under each number.

> LET'S COUNT!
>
> Using the elevator has become a "counting" game for these
> kindergarten children. As they travel in their building from one level
> to another, they watch the numbers change and count out loud—
> both forwards and backwards. As they take turns counting in their
> home languages, the numbers are repeated by all of the children. The
> teacher reports that they get very excited and are proud to showcase
> their counting skills in their home languages.

TABLE 7.3: Sample Chart of Numbers in English, Urdu, and Mandarin

	NUMBERS AND NUMERALS									
Language	1	2	3	4	5	6	7	8	9	10
English	1 one	2 two	3 three	4 four	5 five	6 six	7 seven	8 eight	9 nine	10 ten
Urdu	۱ aik	۲ do	۳ teen	۴ chaar	۵ paanch	۶ chay	۷ saat	۸ aath	۹ nau	۱۰ das
Mandarin	一 yi	二 er	三 san	四 si	五 wu	六 liu	七 qi	八 ba	九 jiu	十 shi

Tips

- Discuss signed numbers with the children, and learn the signs from 1
  to 10 (see chart in Activity 4.3).
- Invite parents and grandparents to join your discussions.
- Prepare "My Numbers" booklets (with 10 blank pages) in which
  children draw pictures of familiar objects—1 object on the first page,
  2 on the second, and so on up to 10—and print the numbers and the
  number words in the classroom and home languages. Invite parents
  to help with the preparation of these booklets.
- As a follow-up activity, read this multi-language counting book with
  the children: Roche, D. (1999). *Can You Count Ten Toes? Count to 10 in
  10 Different Languages*. Boston: Houghton Mifflin.

- Explain the difference between number and numeral to children in the primary grades. A number is an abstract concept, and a numeral is a symbol used to express that number. For example, two, 2, and II are all symbols that express the same number. The difference between a number and its numeral is like the difference between a person and her or his name.

Activity 2.16: Money from Different Countries

This activity will be of interest to kindergarteners and primary graders. Using the world currency website http://www.worldatlas.com/aatlas/infopage/currency.htm, create a money chart that lists the currencies from the children's countries of origin (see Table 7.4). Discuss the two different kinds of currency: paper bills and coins.

TABLE 7.4: Sample Chart of Currencies from Various Countries

LANGUAGE	COUNTRY	PAPER	SYMBOL	COINS
English	Canada	dollars	$	cents
Arabic	Egypt	pound	£	piastre
Farsi	Iran	rial	﷼	toman
Mandarin	China	renminbi	¥	yuan
Polish	Poland	złoty	zl	groszy
Urdu	Pakistan	rupee	₨	paisa

Tips

- Parents can help with the pronunciation of the names of paper bills and coins and can provide additional information about the currency from their country of origin.
- In addition to Canadian play money (available from Scholar's Choice at http://toys.scholarschoice.ca/products/Canadian-Play-Money-p4923/?pstart=1), have real Canadian coins and paper bills on hand to show the children.
- Ask parents to donate paper bills and coins from their country of origin.
- Invite the children to make play money by using pre-cut paper cards for bills and small, round tracing forms for coins.
- Use the homemade paper money in the classroom supermarket (see Activity 2.17).

Activity 2.17: Classroom Supermarket

Discuss shopping for food with the children, encouraging them to share their experiences. Make a plan for setting up a classroom supermarket. With the children, make a list of items that will be needed (e.g., money, cash register, carts, advertisements, shopping baskets, signs), decide on a name for the classroom supermarket, and prepare a sign. Fill the shelves with empty multilingual containers such as boxes, tins, cartons, bags, and plastic bottles brought from home. After you do a safety check for sharp edges, invite the children to sort and organize the containers by language, size, and category. Discuss the roles of those who work in supermarkets, such as the manager, cashiers, and shelf stockers. Use the money from the countries represented in the classroom for the cash register (see Activity 2.16).

Tips

- Make shopping-list notepads by stapling together small sheets of paper.
- Invite parents to contribute empty multilingual containers.

Activity 2.18: Home Language Websites

Many home language websites and video clips especially created for children are available on the Internet. Invite parents to spend classroom time visiting these websites with children who share the same home languages. Prepare a schedule for parental visits and computer use.

Tip

The following websites include interactive activities, games, puzzles, word learning, writing practice, and stories.

- Arabic: http://www.islamicplayground.com/
- Urdu: http://www.ibtada.com/
- Mandarin: http://www.chineseforsmartkids.com/
- Portuguese: http://www.duende.com.br/
- Punjabi: http://learnpunjabi.org/animated_stories.html
- Italian: http://www.disegni.fr/

Theme 3: Linking the Home and Classroom

The activities in Theme 3 link children's family and classroom experiences. In many of the activities, parents and grandparents are invited into the classroom to share their experiences and knowledge.

Activity 3.1: Our Pets

Invite children to share information about their pets. Working with the children, create a chart of who has and does not have pets, the kinds of pets, their names, and their ages. Ask the children which languages they, their siblings, and their parents use to talk to pets. How do the children talk to their pets? Are their pets bilingual? Do the pets understand the classroom language and the home language? If so, how do you know? Do the pets respond the same to each language?

Tip

- Before conducting this activity, familiarize yourself with how different cultures view house pets. You will discover, for example, that not all cultures embrace the dog as a best friend. For information on cross-cultural understanding of pets, see Gray and Young (2011).

Activity 3.2: Grandparents in the Classroom

 Grandparents are special people for many young children. Including grandmothers and grandfathers in classroom activities will provide an opportunity for them to share knowledge about their counties of origin. They can also serve as home language models. Prepare a letter of invitation that includes a schedule of days, times, and class activities. For example, grandparents can participate in some of the Theme 2 activities described previously.

Tip

- Appendix 7.C lists picture books about grandparents. Librarians will help you find more. As you (or grandparents) share these books, encourage the children to talk about their grandparents.

Activity 3.3: Grandpa, Grandma, How Old Are You?

With the help of grandparents, create a chart that documents the ages of children, grandfathers, and grandmothers. Young children love big numbers and will find this activity enjoyable. Be sure to use the classroom language colour codes. In the two examples, information about grandfathers (Table 7.5) and grandmothers (Table 7.6) is presented in separate charts.

TABLE 7.5: Ages of Children and Grandfathers

GRANDCHILD'S NAME	AGE	GRANDFATHER'S NAME	GRANDFATHER IN DIFFERENT LANGUAGES	AGE
Amira	5		Arabic:	
Elizabeth	4		English:	
Agnieczka	5		Polish:	

TABLE 7.6: Ages of Children and Grandmothers

GRANDCHILD'S NAME	AGE	GRANDMOTHER'S NAME	GRANDMOTHER IN DIFFERENT LANGUAGES	AGE
Amira	5		Arabic:	
Elizabeth	4		English:	
Agnieczka	5		Polish:	

Activity 3.4: Grandparents' Stories

Children are often intrigued by their grandparents' life stories. It is a good idea, then, to invite grandparents to the classroom to share some of their life stories with the children. Older children can develop a series of interview questions designed to get information about the life stories of grandmothers and grandfathers. Ask them to conduct an "interview" using a tape recorder. They can then create a book entitled *My Grandparents*, which will include responses to the questions (in the classroom and home languages), illustrations, and photos. Children who do not have grandparents can interview older relatives, neighbours, or close family friends.

Tip

Here are some sample interview questions:

- When were you born?
- Where were you born?
- Where did you live while you were growing up?
- What did your mother call you?
- What languages did you speak as you were growing up?
- What was your favourite toy as a child?

- What did you wear?
- What was your favourite food?
- Did your family have a car? A TV? A computer? A cell phone? A dishwasher?
- Did you have to do any chores? What were they?
- What types of things did you and your family do for fun?
- Did you go to school?
- Did you like school?
- Were you a good student?
- How did you get to school each morning?
- What do you remember about your teachers, your classroom?
- What types of games did you play with your friends?

Activity 3.5: Creating a Family Tree

To help children better understand their place in the family, introduce the concept of genealogy, the study of families. In your discussion, describe the features of a family tree and review or introduce relevant terms such as family, generation, family name, given name, mother, father, brother, sister, grandchild, grandparents, paternal, maternal, relative, grandmother, grandfather, aunt, uncle, and cousin. Invite grandparents, parents, or relatives to help children create a family tree. Encourage the children to add illustrations and photos to their family trees.

Tips

- Encourage grandparents, parents, or relatives to add names in the home language.
- The following website offers suggestions and templates for creating family trees with children: http://www.dltk-bible.com/genesis/families/my_family_tree.htm.

Activity 3.6: Come Cook with Us

Invite parents to share a simple recipe with the class. Prepare a recipe card on which parents can list, in the classroom and in their home languages, the name of the dish, the country of origin, the ingredients, the required utensils, instructions, and preparation time. Prepare a cooking schedule for parents to come and cook with the children.

Tips

Before cooking in the classroom

- discuss cooking safety,

- display and discuss the recipe card prepared by the parent,
- go shopping with the children to buy the ingredients for the recipe,
- make a list of ingredients in both languages, and
- encourage parents to engage the children in the preparation of the dish.

Activity 3.7: Placemats

Make blank placemats (18" x 12") from sturdy white paper that the children can decorate with illustrations or magazine cut-outs of food items. Encourage them to label the food items in the classroom and home languages. Laminate completed placemats, and use them during snack time or when sharing dishes prepared in the classroom.

Activity 3.8: *Bon Appétit*

Different mealtime practices exist across cultures and languages. Some groups recite or sing prayers before and after a meal while others wish each other a "good appetite" before starting to eat. For example, the French wish each other *bon appétit*, while Germans say *Guten Appetit* before the start of a meal. Before you share the dish prepared in Activity 3.6, ask the children what is said in their home as they begin and end a meal. Encourage all of the children to repeat the contributions.

Tip

- For a list of translations of *bon appétit* see http://www.omniglot. com/language/phrases/bonappetit.htm.

....

Theme 4: Bringing the Outside World into the Classroom
....

In these activities, different language practices are explored, discussed, and compared.

Activity 4.1: Telephone Manners

Telephone culture is very different across languages. Invite parents into the classroom to explain the telephone manners of their language. Using a toy cell phone, invite children to practice telephone manners in different languages.

Tip

- The following website lists telephone manners of different language groups: http://www.netjeff.com/humor/item.cgi?file=HelloOnTele phoneWorldwide.

Activity 4.2: Neighbourhood Signs

To prepare children for a neighbourhood walk, initiate a discussion about their own neighbourhood, the services offered in it, and its shops and signs. As you walk around the child care centre or school neighbourhood, ask the children to look for signs in different languages. Point out the different places where signs are found, such as storefronts, awnings, trucks, cars, newspaper boxes, bus stops, posts, and stand-alone signs. Photograph the signs you encounter. Once back in the classroom, transfer your photos onto the computer and download them. Create a sign book with the children, in which signs are sorted by function (traffic, street name, kind of store) and translated into home languages.

Tips

- It is important to take the time to explore the school or childcare centre neighbourhood *before* setting out with the children on a neighbourhood walk. Familiarity with the physical layout of the community and its available services and resources will allow you to plan your walk and plan follow-up activities.
- Prearranging visits, so members of the community can take the time to explain the services they offer and which languages they use, will make your walk more meaningful.

Activity 4.3: Sign Language

It is important for children to understand that some people cannot hear or speak. Some of these people use listening devices or hearing aids, but others do not. Instead of using their ears to listen and their mouths to speak, they use their eyes to watch and their hands, fingers, and faces to talk. An age-appropriate discussion about non-verbal communication will help children understand this.

FIGURE 7.8: American Sign Language Alphabet and Numbers from 1 to 10

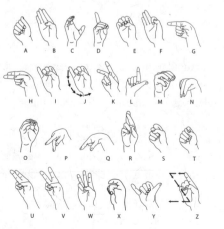

FIGURE 7.9: American Sign Language, Basic Signs

"Hello"   "Good Bye"   "Yes"   "No"

"Thanks"   "You're Welcome"   "Please"   "Sorry"

Enlarge, copy, and display Figures 7.8 and 7.9 in the language centre. With the children, practice spelling their names using the American Sign Language alphabet (Figure 7.8).

SOME SIGN LANGUAGE FACTS TO SHARE WITH CHILDREN

- Not all people are able to use oral or spoken language.
- Many Deaf people use sign language.
- People are not able to hear for many reasons. Some are born that way.
- Sign language is a language of the hands and face.
- There is a one-hand (or finger) alphabet for spelling individual letters of words.
- Letters are signed with the dominant hand and with the palm facing the viewer.
- There are many signs for whole words, and making one of these signs means the same as speaking the word.
- In addition to finger spelling and hand signs, people can use gestures, body language, face movements, and lips to communicate.
- There are different sign languages all over the world, just as there are different spoken languages: American Sign Language, French Sign Language, Taiwan Sign Language, Thai Sign Language.
- Sign languages are complete, complex languages.
- ASL (American Sign Language) is the first language of many Deaf North Americans.

Tips

- Appendix 7.D lists books about sign language. Your librarian can help you find more.

- Together with the children, learn the signs in Figure 7.9 and use them in everyday classroom interactions.
- See the "Fun Facts about ASL" brochure (http://www.deaf-kids. org/IND/documents/PDFASLBroch.pdf) and information from the Deaf Culture Centre on how to refer to people who cannot hear (http://www.deafculturecentre.ca/Public/Default.aspx?I=295&n=H earing+Impaired%3F).

WE KNOW SIGN LANGUAGE!

My grade-one children are familiar with basic signs. We use them in class daily. One morning, two girls look at an ASL book together. They try new signs and ask each other what the signs mean. They come to me with their newly learned signs and state, "Bet you don't know this one!" They proudly demonstrate the new signs and tell me that I haven't taught them everything that's in the book—which, of course, is true!

Activity 4.4: International Mother Language Day

In 1999, the United Nations Educational, Scientific, and Cultural Organization (UNESCO) proclaimed February 21 as International Mother Language Day (IMLD). The purpose of this day is "to promote the preservation and protection of all languages used by peoples of the world" and "to promote unity in diversity and international understanding, through multilingualism and multiculturalism."

There are a number of activities that could be undertaken around IMLD. For example, you could download the IMLD poster from the UNESCO website (http://www.un.org/en/events/motherlanguageday/) and display it in the language centre. Information about IMLD and valuable resources for educators can also be found on this website. Invite parents to help in the preparation of your own classroom IMLD posters. Discuss what should be included on the poster. Display the completed posters in the language centre. With parents and children, plan a classroom celebration of languages on February 21.

Activity 4.5: Sounds around Us

Environmental sounds are reproduced differently across countries. For example, the sound of a rooster in English is *cock-a-doodle-doo*; in French, it is *cocorico*; in Dutch, *kukeleku*; in German, *kikeriki*; and in Ukrainian, it is *kukuriku*. Children find this exciting and funny. On the website http://www.bzzzpeek.com/, you will find the sounds of animals, reptiles, cars, insects, and birds produced by children from more than 20 countries. Download the website onto the class computer and invite the children to attempt to reproduce and compare the different sounds.

Theme 5: Sharing Books and Newspapers with Children

Theme 5 activities include book discussions and reading with children. Special attention is paid to sharing and creating dual language books with children and families.

Activity 5.1: Book Talk

Talk to the children about books. Describe the main features of a book, such as author or authors, illustrator and illustrations, publisher, front and back cover, table of contents, text, font, and page numbers. Discuss the different kinds of books (story, information). Explain the use of two-language dictionaries, asking parents to provide samples.

Tips

- Have samples of different kinds of books on hand.
- Invite the school librarian to talk to the children about the importance and care of books.
- Arrange visits to the school library.
- Ask the school librarian about books in home languages.
- Encourage children to bring their favourite books to the classroom.
- Encourage parents to read books in home languages to individual children or to the group.

Activity 5.2: Story Time

The language centre is a good place for story time. As you read books in the classroom language, invite children to provide home language translations for single words and phrases (e.g., Azin, how do you say "water" in your language?). Initially, children may hesitate, but when they understand that their home languages have a place in the classroom, they will eagerly contribute and participate. Invite parents and community members to come to the language centre to share stories and provide translations.

SAYING DOG IN MY LANGUAGE!

After numerous activities that encourage and showcase home languages, six-year-old Dima contributes the following during story time: "In Russian, dog is sobachka."

Activity 5.3: Shared Family Reading[1]

This activity brings together families and children to share books written in the classroom and in home languages. Reading sessions are held in the classroom during school hours or in the evening, and are facilitated by EC practitioners who provide parents with information about the importance of literacy.

Tip

- For suggestions on organizing and conducting reading sessions with parents consult *Family Literacy in Action: A Guide for Literacy Program Facilitators* by Pelletier, Hipfner-Boucher, and Doyle (2010).

Activity 5.4: Visiting the Public Library

Most children's rooms in public libraries accept groups of children for story time. Before you take the children to the library, visit on your own to introduce yourself to the librarian and inquire about multilingual children's books.

MULTILINGUAL LIBRARY COLLECTIONS

Whenever I conduct a tour of the children's department, whether it's with a Grade 2 or Grade 4 class, I always make a point of stopping at our multilingual collection and asking the kids if they speak a language other than English. Usually 85–90 per cent of the hands go up. The kids are always excited to talk about where they've come from and the languages they speak—their faces quite literally light up. We live in a country that welcomes and celebrates diversity, and that extends to linguistic diversity.

—John Lukasik, Children's Librarian

Tips

- With the help of the children's librarian, make a list of books in the home languages represented in your classroom.
- Share this list with parents.

....

1 This activity is based on the *School-Based Family Literacy Intervention Program* (Pelletier, 2011; Zhang, 2009).

- Invite parents and grandparents to visit the library with the class, and encourage them to read to small groups of children.
- Encourage the children to join the public library and borrow books in the languages of both the classroom and the home.

Activity 5.5: Reading Newspapers

Newspapers are an inexpensive and valuable classroom resource that can support children's multilingual and multi-literacy learning. They can also introduce, reinforce, enrich, and extend content taught in the classroom. Select a "newspaper day," a day and time (weekly) to talk about and read newspapers. Discuss the features of the daily newspaper with children, such as its name, size, sections, numbered pages, black and coloured print, the size of the print, advertisements, and photographs. Also discuss the processes involved in getting the newspaper to the reader, e.g., printing, home delivery, and newspaper boxes.

Tips

- Ask children to bring newspapers written in their home languages to the classroom.
- Invite parents to discuss and share the main features of these newspapers.
- Select age-appropriate sections of the newspapers to discuss and read with children.
- Contact your daily newspaper to arrange a class visit.

Activity 5.6: Creating a Multilingual Newspaper

Using a local newspaper as a guide, create a multilingual classroom newspaper. Decide on a name for the newspaper. Select newspaper staff: editor, journalists, and photographers. Think about and plan the paper's size and number of pages. Plan article topics (e.g., classroom events and trips, visitors, special days, celebrations), and include illustrations and photos. Working with the children and parents, prepare the layout. Invite parents to prepare a home language section. Read the completed newspaper aloud with the children. Invite parents to read the sections in the home languages.

Dual Language Book Activities: Introduction

What Are Dual Language Books?

Dual language books for young children include colourful illustrations and short text in two languages. Text in the classroom language is found on one page and text in a home language is on the facing page. Dual language books can be shared with individual children or read to a group by the EC practitioner, a parent, or an older sibling. Most school and public libraries have collections of dual language books.

Benefits of Dual Language Books

Everyone stands to benefit from dual language books. They provide a "comfort zone" for newly arrived immigrant children, helping them to transition into the classroom. They bridge home and classroom languages and help children take pride in their home languages. Dual language books provide children with opportunities to showcase their home language skills and to develop their language awareness, as they notice language similarities and differences. These books help increase vocabulary in the home language and in the classroom language. They also help families feel recognized and welcomed in the classroom. Dual language books provide opportunities for parents and grandparents to take an active role in their child's (or grandchild's) learning by sharing their language knowledge with all children.

Monolingual children also benefit from dual language books. Listening to stories in new languages helps them develop an understanding of linguistic differences and provides opportunities to explore other languages.

And, finally, dual language books serve as a reminder that, to promote bilingualism, the EC practitioner does not need to be a speaker of children's home languages. Dual language books are an effective way of bringing home languages into the classroom and are a natural and easy way to partner with families.

Activity 5.7: Reading Dual Language Books

Although dual language books are found in most classrooms, EC practitioners are often unsure how best to use them with children. What follows is a three-part "how to" guide for reading a dual language book with young children. The book used in the example is the English–Urdu version of a popular story *The Very Hungry Caterpillar* (written and illustrated by Eric Carle). For information on the English version of this book, see the Penguin website dedicated to it (http://us.penguingroup.com/static/pages/features/hungrycaterpillar/index.html). Dual language versions are available from Mantra Lingua (http://www.mantralingua.com/usa/home.php).

Part One: Introducing the Dual Language Book

Hold up the book in front of the children and explain how it will be read. Here is a sample introduction:

We have a story today about a hungry caterpillar. He was just as hungry as we are at lunchtime…. As you can see (pointing), the story is in English and in another language. That other language is Urdu. Urdu is Sabirah's, Johara's, and Tahir's language. The English words are here (pointing), and the Urdu words are here (pointing). I'll read the story in English, and Tahir's dad will read it in Urdu. Listen carefully for the fruit the caterpillar gobbles up!

Part Two: Reading a Dual Language Book

There are two ways to read a dual language book to children, in its entirety or page by page.

1. Reading the entire book:
   - The EC practitioner reads the entire story in the classroom language. During the reading, children are encouraged to recall the names of the days and the kind of fruit the caterpillar ate.
   - Following the reading in the classroom language, Tahir's dad reads the entire book in Urdu—the other language in the dual language book. Because this is an unfamiliar language to most of the children, he points to the words and reads slowly and clearly. Following the procedure used by the EC practitioner, Tahir's dad brings attention to the names of the days and the kinds of fruit the caterpillar ate.
2. Page-by-page reading:
   - Another way to read the English-Urdu dual language book is to read one page at a time. This means that the EC practitioner's reading of one page (in the classroom language) is followed by the reading of the same page in Urdu.

Part Three: Follow-Up Activity

Think of ways to include home languages in activities that follow the reading of the dual language book. For example, as the children recall the days of the week, the fruit, and the quantity that the caterpillar ate, the EC practitioner records their responses on a chart (see Table 7.7). Following this, Tahir's dad, who read the story in Urdu, can include the Urdu words in the three columns: the days of the week, the names of the fruit that the caterpillar ate, and the number of each fruit eaten.

TABLE 7.7: Dual Language Book Follow-Up Activity

WHAT THE CATERPILLAR ATE AND WHEN					
Days of the week		Fruit		How many?	
English	Urdu	English	Urdu	English	Urdu
Monday		apple		1	
Tuesday		pear		2	
Wednesday		plum		3	
Thursday		strawberry		4	
Friday		orange		5	

Tips

- The following two websites offer a wide range of dual language books for purchase:
  - http://www.languagelizard.com/
  - http://fareasternbooks.com/
- For additional information on the benefits of dual language books, see Appelt (2008); Bismilla, Cummins, Leoni, and Sandhu (2006); Edwards and Walker (1995); Ernst-Slavit, Moore, and Maloney (2002); Ma (2004, 2008); and Taylor, Bernhard, Garg, and Cummins (2008).

Activity 5.8: Creating Dual Language Books

In addition to reading dual language books, children and their parents can be encouraged to create individual or group books that include illustrations and text in two languages. These books can be related to classroom themes or based on personal experiences. They can be prepared in the classroom or at home. Dual language books can include simple illustrations accompanied by language labels, or they can be simple stories (e.g., *All about Me*), with two-language text dictated by younger children and printed (by hand or computer) by parents. Older children can write the dual language text on their own.

I'LL MAKE ONE IN MANDARIN!

After completing his "Number Book" in English, a four-year-old Mandarin-speaking boy announces to the EC practitioner, "Now I'll make one in Mandarin, OK?"

Tips

- Make dual language book preparation a regular classroom activity that can be extended into children's homes.

- Keep parents informed and updated about classroom themes and activities.
- Have materials (lined, unlined, white and coloured paper, markers, crayons, pencils) on hand for children to construct their dual language books.
- Have bilingual dictionaries on hand.
- Encourage children to refer to the language charts (see Chapter 5) as they prepare their dual language books.
- With the children, prepare a list of topics for dual language books, such as numbers, colours, shapes, seasons, classroom items and objects, my house, my family, and my country.
- Invite students from higher grades to come to your classroom to help children create dual language books.
- Send blank dual language books home to be completed with parents and older siblings.
- Keep a record of the number of dual language books completed by each child.
- Laminate completed dual language books.
- Ask children to read their completed dual language books to the class or to small groups.
- Place completed dual language books in the classroom library—in the appropriate box.
- Invite *all* children to create dual language books.
- Encourage monolingual children to include in their dual language books a language spoken by a special friend.
- Invite the French language teacher to help monolingual children prepare English-French dual language books.
- A variety of resources are available to help guide your book-making activities:

Websites
- "Let's Book It," *Vicki Blackwell* (http://www.vickiblackwell.com/makingbooks/index.htm)
- "Making Class Books in Kindergarten," *Nellie Edge* (http://www.nellieedge.com/articles_resources/MakingClassBooks.htm)
- *Family Treasures and Grandma's Soup: A Dual Language Book Project* (http://www.duallanguageproject.com/index.html)
- *Thornwood Public School: Dual Language Showcase* (http://www.thornwoodps.ca/dual/index.htm)

Books

- Fairfax, B., & García, A. (1998). *Read! Write! and Publish! Making books in the classroom*. Huntington Beach, CA: Creative Teaching Press.
- Ada, A.F., & Campoy, I. (2005). *Authors in the classroom: A transformative education process*. Boston: Allyn and Bacon.

A Final Word on LAP Activities

After you have tried a few LAP activities, you will discover new ways of adding home languages to your curriculum. In this way, you will enrich the lives of *all* children, not only those who are growing in two languages. Your open door and your acceptance of all languages will help all children develop an understanding, acceptance, and appreciation of language differences.

Key Points

1. LAP activities
   - cover a wide range of topics and subject areas;
   - are organized thematically;
   - are conducted in the classroom language and include a home language component;
   - require careful preparation and planning;
   - can be adapted, adjusted, and extended to match the developmental level and the interests of the children;
   - will positively affect the personal and social development of *all* children;
   - will help all children develop science and math skills;
   - will promote an understanding of local and global community life; and
   - will help all children develop skills in the following four areas of the classroom language: oral communication, reading, writing, and media literacy.
2. Some LAP activities are conducted in home languages.
3. Many LAP activities require the help of families.
4. The home language component of LAP activities will help immigrant children improve their skills in four areas of the home language: oral communication, reading, writing, and media literacy.
5. The inclusion of French (or English in francophone classrooms)

in selected activities will help all children develop an awareness and appreciation of Canada's two official languages and will serve as a stepping stone to children's later French or English classroom instruction.

6. EC practitioners are *promoters*—and not teachers—of home languages. The main responsibility for the development of oral communication, reading, writing, and media literacy skills in the home language lies in the home.

Group Activities

1. Extending LAP Activities

Select five activities found in this chapter and think of ways they can be extended.

Example 1

The "Hello-Goodbye" chart (Theme 2) can be extended to include other phrases, such as "Thank you, You're welcome"; "Good morning, Good evening, Good night"; "How are you?"; "How old are you?"; "How are you feeling?"; "Can I help you?"; "I love you"; "You are my friend"; "Stop, Go"; and "Come here, Go away."

Example 2

After reading *The Very Hungry Caterpillar* in English and in Urdu (Theme 5), show a YouTube version of the story to the children (see, for example, http://wn.com/The_Very_Hungry_Caterpillar). Turn off the sound, and invite them to narrate the story in their home languages.

2. What Else Can Be Done?

Think of five ways to add a home language component to your curriculum. Go to the text box entitled "It's a Sevivon!" on page 117. Read it and discuss the following:

- What is your response to the EC practitioner's actions?
- If you were confronted with this situation, what would you do?
- Think of five ways to extend Joshua's learning of Hebrew in the classroom.
- How could you engage Joshua's parents in the classroom?

APPENDIX 7.A

LAP Activities by Theme

Theme 1: Charting Home Languages
Activity 1.1: The Sign-In Book
Activity 1.2: The Colours of Our Home Languages
Activity 1.3: The Colour of My Home Language
Activity 1.4: Our Home Language Book
Activity 1.5: Our Home Language Tree
Activity 1.6: Bilingual Name Cards
Activity 1.7: Home Language Graphs
Activity 1.8: Sorting Classroom Books by Language
Activity 1.9: Country, Flag, and Language Chart

Theme 2: Using Home Languages in the Classroom
Activity 2.1: Singing in Home Languages
Activity 2.2: How Do You Say "Music" in Your Language?
Activity 2.3: Morning Puzzler
Activity 2.4: Calendar Time
Activity 2.5: Calendars from Home
Activity 2.6: I Love Different Languages—Do You?
Activity 2.7: Language Ball

Word Learning Activities
Activity 2.8: "What Do You See?"
Activity 2.9: Word Cards
Activity 2.10: Hello-Goodbye Chart
Activity 2.11: Happy Birthday Chart
Activity 2.12: Bilingual Greeting Cards
Activity 2.13: Newspaper Letter and Word Hunt
Activity 2.14: Our Alphabets and Writing Systems
Activity 2.15: Numbers in Home Languages
Activity 2.16: Money from Different Countries
Activity 2.17: Classroom Supermarket
Activity 2.18: Home Language Websites

Theme 3: Linking the Home and Classroom
Activity 3.1: Our Pets
Activity 3.2: Grandparents in the Classroom

Activity 3.3: Grandpa, Grandma, How Old Are You?
Activity 3.4: Grandparents' Stories
Activity 3.5: Creating a Family Tree
Activity 3.6: Come Cook with Us
Activity 3.7: Placemats
Activity 3.8: *Bon Appétit*

Theme 4: Bringing the Outside World into the Classroom

Activity 4.1: Telephone Manners
Activity 4.2: Neighbourhood Signs
Activity 4.3: Sign Language
Activity 4.4: International Mother Language Day
Activity 4.5: Sounds around Us

Theme 5: Sharing Books and Newspapers with Children

Activity 5.1: Book Talk
Activity 5.2: Story Time
Activity 5.3: Shared Family Reading
Activity 5.4: Visiting the Public Library
Activity 5.5: Reading Newspapers
Activity 5.6: Creating a Multilingual Newspaper

Dual Language Book Activities

Activity 5.7: Reading Dual Language Books
Activity 5.8: Creating Dual Language Books

APPENDIX 7.B

....

Books about Writing Systems

....

Bajaj, V., & Crawford, R.R. (2011). *T is for Taj Mahal: An Indian alphabet*. Chelsea, MI: Sleeping Bear Press.

Grodin, E. (2008). *C is for ciao: An Italy alphabet*. Chelsea, MI: Sleeping Bear Press.

Pitchall, C. (2003). *My world alphabet*. Markham, ON: Scholastic.

Rahman, U., & Prodeesta, D. (2009). *B is for Bangladesh*. London: Frances Lincoln.

Scillian, D. (2003). *P is for passport: A world alphabet*. Chelsea, MI: Sleeping Bear Press.

APPENDIX 7.C

Books about Grandparents

Crystal, B. (2006). *Grandpa's little one*. New York: Harper Collins.

DePaola, T. (1981). *Now one foot, now the other*. New York: Putnam.

DePaola, T. (1998). *Nana upstairs & Nana downstairs*. New York: Putnam.

Dorros, A. (1991). *Abuela*. New York: Dutton Children's Books.

Johnson, A. (1990). *When I am old with you*. New York: Orchard Books.

Juster, N. (2005). *Hello, goodbye window*. New York: Hyperion Books for Children.

Lamarche, J. (2000). *The raft*. New York: Lothrop, Lee & Sheppard Books.

Lloyd-James, S., & Emberley, M. (2008). *The ultimate guide to grandmas and grandpas!* New York: Harper Collins.

Martin, M.P. (1971). *Annie and the old one*. Boston: Little, Brown.

Mayer, M. (1983). *Just grandma and me*. New York: Golden Press.

Minarik, H.E. (1961). *Little bear's visit*. New York: Harper & Row.

Rylant, C. (1982). *When I was young in the mountains*. New York: Dutton.

Spyri, J. (2006). *Heidi*. New York: Sterling Publishers.

APPENDIX 7.D

Books about Sign Language

Blatchford, C.H. (1998). *Going with the flow*. Minneapolis: Carolrhoda Books.

Booth, B.D. (1991). *Mandy*. New York: Lothrop, Lee & Shepard Books.

Heelan, R.J. (2002). *Can you hear a rainbow? The story of a deaf boy named Chris*. Atlanta: Peachtree Publishers.

Levi, D. (1989). *A very special friend*. Washington, DC: Kendall Green Publications.

Litchfield, A.B. (1976). *A button in her ear*. Chicago, IL: Albert Whitman & Company.

Wah, J. (1999). *Rosa's parrot*. Dallas, TX: Whispering Coyote Press.

LOOKING AHEAD

LAP gives young immigrant children the attention they need. Developed as a response to numerous requests from EC practitioners and the widespread monolingual practices found in today's classrooms, LAP views immigrant children as bilinguals in the making, promotes their home languages, and fosters multilingual, multi-literate, and multicultural awareness in all children. Rooted in dynamic bilingualism, LAP acknowledges the language and literacy needs of young immigrant children and views classrooms as dynamic linguistically complex ecosystems where all languages grow, blend, and flourish.

This book provides a guide to working with young immigrant children using a new classroom practice called "Linguistically Appropriate Practice" or LAP. Part I presents important background information. It reaffirms the presence of immigrant children in urban classrooms, portrays their language circumstance, gives an overview of current classroom practices, and gives readers the theoretical grounding of LAP. Part II sets the stage for the launch of LAP. It invites EC practitioners to accept the LAP challenge and shows them how to prepare the classroom for LAP, transition immigrant children from the home to the classroom, introduce new immigrant children, partner with families, use home languages in the classroom, and document language and literacy classroom behaviours. In Part III specific LAP activities are outlined and their benefits are explained. The activities cover a wide range of topics, are divided into five themes, and can be adapted, adjusted and extended to match the developmental level and the interests of the children.

The closing LAP message looks ahead to the future. It appeals to those working with young immigrant children to turn their attention to this ever-increasing population.

EC practitioners are encouraged to

- think about the classroom practices they adopt in their work with immigrant children,
- adopt LAP as a team enterprise,
- share ideas and discuss strategies,
- develop and create additional ways of bringing home languages into classrooms,
- build relationships with families and language communities, and
- become advocates of the importance and benefits of bilingualism.

Policy makers are urged to

- provide an equitable, research-based policy framework for working with young immigrant children, and
- provide resources for EC practitioners to implement LAP.

Researchers are invited to provide much-needed data on the following three topics:

- the transition of immigrant children from the home to the classroom,
- immigrant children's stages of classroom language learning, and
- the effects of translanguaging on dual language learning.

EC education programs are urged to include the following in their courses of study:

- the language circumstance of young immigrant children,
- dynamic bilingualism,
- the language and literacy needs of young immigrant children,
- building partnerships with immigrant parents, and
- promoting multilingualism and multi-literacy.

And finally … my journey to know and understand young immigrant children, which led to the preparation of this book, is far from over. I know that, as I continue to interact with *real* children and with those who care for and teach them, I will discover and learn even more. And when this happens, perhaps I will be ready to add a stroke or two to the language portrait painted in this book.

REFERENCES

Ada, A.F., & Campoy, I. (2005). *Authors in the classroom: A transformative education process.* Boston: Allyn and Bacon.

Appelt, L. (2008, March). Dual-language books: Addressing linguistic and cultural diversity in French immersion classrooms. Paper presented at the Graduate Student Language and Literacy Conference, University of Victoria, Vancouver, BC. Retrieved from http://web.uvic.ca/~literacy/confproced.html.

Ashworth, M., & Wakefield, H.P. (2004). *Teaching the world's children: ESL for ages three to seven.* Toronto: Pippin Publishers.

Au, K. (2006). *Multicultural issues and literacy achievement.* Mahwah, NJ: Lawrence Erlbaum Associates.

Baker, C. (2006). *Foundations of bilingual education and bilingualism.* Clevedon, UK: Multilingual Matters.

Berthelsen, D., & Brownlee, J. (2007). Working with toddlers in childcare: Practitioners, beliefs about their role. *Early Childhood Research Quarterly, 22*(3), 347–362. http://dx.doi.org/10.1016/j.ecresq.2006.12.002

Bialystok, E. (1987a). Influences of bilingualism on metalinguistic development. *Second Language Research, 3*(2), 154–166. http://dx.doi.org/10.1177/026765838700300205

Bialystok, E. (1987b). Words as things: Development of word concept by bilingual children. *Studies in Second Language Learning, 9*(2), 133–140. http://dx.doi.org/10.1017/S0272263100000437

Bialystok, E. (1991). *Language processing in bilingual children.* Cambridge: Cambridge University Press. http://dx.doi.org/10.1017/CBO9780511620652

Bialystok, E. (1992). Attentional control in children's meta linguistic performance and measures of field independence. *Developmental Psychology, 28*(4), 654–664. http://dx.doi.org/10.1037/0012-1649.28.4.654

Bialystok, E. (1997). Effects of bilingualism and biliteracy on children's emerging concepts of print. *Developmental Psychology, 33*(3), 429–440. http://dx.doi.org/10.1037/0012-1649.33.3.429

Bialystok, E. (2001a). *Bilingualism in development: Language, literacy, and cognition.* New York: Cambridge University Press. http://dx.doi.org/10.1017/CBO9780511605963

Bialystok, E. (2001b). Metalinguistic aspects of bilingual processing. *Annual Review of Applied Linguistics, 21,* 169–181. http://dx.doi.org/10.1017/S0267190501000101

Bialystok, E., & Martin, M.M. (2004). Attention and inhibition in bilingual children: Evidence from the dimensional change card sort task. *Developmental Science, 7*(3), 325–339. http://dx.doi.org/10.1111/j.1467-7687.2004.00351.x Medline:15595373

Bialystok, E., & Shapiro, D. (2005). Ambiguous benefits: The effect of bilingualism on reversing ambiguous figures. *Developmental Science, 8*(6), 595–604. http://dx.doi.org/10.1111/j.1467-7687.2005.00451.x Medline:16246250

Bismilla, V., Cummins, J. Leoni, L. & Sandhu, P. (2006). *Incorporation of students' first language into classroom instruction: Effects on self-esteem and academic engagement* (Case Study Report). The Multiliteracy Project, Department of Language and Literacy Education, University of British Columbia, Vancouver, BC.

Bohan-Baker, M., & Little, P.M.D. (2002, April). *The transition to kindergarten: A review of current research and promising practices to involve families* (Research Report). Cambridge, MA: Harvard Family Research Project. Retrieved from http://www.hfrp.org/content/download/1165/48670/file/bohan.pdf.

Canadian Children: Journal of the Canadian Association for Young Children. (2001–2010). Vancouver, BC: Canadian Association for Young Children. Retrieved from http://www.cayc.ca/index.html

Canadian Immigration Newsletter. (2008, August). More immigrants looking to smaller Canadian cities for a place to call home. *CIC News.* Retrieved from http://www.cicnews.com/2008/08/immigrants-smaller-canadian-cities-place-call-home-08676.html

Canadian Oxford dictionary. (2004). Don Mills, ON: Oxford University Press Canada.

Carle, E. (1969). *The very hungry caterpillar.* New York: World Publishing Company.

Chang, H.N. (1993). *Affirming children's roots: Cultural and linguistic diversity in early care and education.* San Francisco, CA: California Tomorrow.

Chumak-Horbatsch, R. (2004). Linguistic diversity in early childhood education: Working with linguistically and culturally diverse children. *Canadian Children, 29*(2), 20–24.

Chumak-Horbatsch, R. (2006). Mmmm … I like English! Linguistic behaviours of Ukrainian-English bilingual children. *Psychology of Language and Communication, 10*(2), 3–25.

Chumak-Horbatsch, R. (2008). Early bilingualism: Children of immigrants in an English-language childcare centre. *Psychology of Language and Communication, 12*(1), 3–27. http://dx.doi.org/10.2478/v10057-008-0001-2

Chumak-Horbatsch, R. (2010). Toronto childcare centres: A language profile. In B. Bokus (Ed.), *Studies in the psychology of language and communication* (pp. 289–307). Warsaw: Matrix.

City of Toronto. (2012). *Toronto's Racial Diversity.* Retrieved from http://www.toronto.ca/toronto_facts/diversity.htm.

Collicelli, C. (2001). *Child Immigration Project: Final report* (Targeted Socio-Economic Research No. SOE2-CT98-1109). Brussels: European Commission.

Colomé, A. (2001). Lexical activation in bilinguals' speech production: Language-specific or language-independent? *Journal of Memory and Language, 45*(4), 721–736. http://dx.doi.org/10.1006/jmla.2001.2793

Creese, A., & Blackledge, A. (2010). Translanguaging in the bilingual classroom: A pedagogy for learning and teaching? *Modern Language Journal, 94*(1), 103–115. http://dx.doi.org/10.1111/j.1540-4781.2009.00986.x

Creese, A., & Martin, P. (2006). Linguistic diversity in the classroom: An ecological perspective. *NALDIC Quarterly, 3*(3), 27–32.

Cummins, J. (1979). *Cognitive/academic language proficiency, linguistic interdependence, the optimum age question and some other matters* (Working Papers on Bilingualism No. 19). Toronto: Ontario Institute for Studies in Education, Bilingual Education Project. (ERIC Document Reproduction Service No. ED184334.)

Cummins, J. (1981). The role of primary language development in promoting educational success for language minority students. In California State Department of Education (Ed.), *Schooling and language minority students: A theoretical framework* (pp. 3–49). Sacramento, CA: California State Department of Education. (ERIC Document Reproduction Service No. ED249773.)

Cummins, J. (2000). *Language, power, and pedagogy: Bilingual children in the crossfire.* Clevedon, UK: Multilingual Matters.

Cummins, J. (2001a). Bilingual children's mother tongue: Why is it important for education? *Sprogforum, 7*(19), 15–20.

Cummins, J. (2001b). *Negotiating identities: Education for empowerment in a diverse society* (2nd ed.). Los Angeles, CA: California Association for Bilingual Education.

Edwards, V., & Walker, S. (1995). *Building bridges: Multilingual resources for children.* Clevedon, UK: Multilingual Matters.

Ernst-Slavit, G., Moore, M., & Maloney, C. (2002). Changing lives: Teaching English and literature to ESL students. *Journal of Adolescent & Adult Literacy, 48*(2), 118–128.

Erwin-Tripp, S. (1974). Is second language learning like the first? *TESOL Quarterly, 8*(2), 111–127. http://dx.doi.org/10.2307/3585535

Eurydice. (2009). *Integrating immigrant children into schools in Europe.* Brussels: European Commission. Retrieved from http://eacea.ec.europa.eu/education/eurydice/documents/thematic_reports/101EN.pdf

Fairfax, B., & Garcia, A. (1998). *Read! Write! and Publish! Making books in the classroom.* Huntington Beach, CA: Creative Teaching Press.

García, O. (2009a). Education, multilingualism, and translanguaging in the 21st century. In T. Skutnabb-Kangas, R. Phillipson, A.K. Mohanty, & M. Panda (Eds.). *Multicultural education for social justice: Globalizing the local* (pp. 140–158). Bristol, UK: Multilingual Matters.

García, O. (2009b). Emergent bilinguals and TESOL: What's in a name? *TESOL Quarterly 43*(2): 322–326. Special issue edited by Shelley Taylor.

García, O. (2009c). *Bilingual education in the 21st century: A global perspective*. Oxford: Wiley-Blackwell.

García, O. (2010). Latino language practices and literacy education in the U.S. In M. Farr, L. Seloni, & J. Song (Eds.), *Ethnolinguistic diversity and education: Langauge, literacy, and culture* (pp. 193–211). New York: Routledge.

García, O. (2011). The translanguaging of Latino kindergarteners. In K. Potowski & J. Rothman (Eds.), *Bilingual youth: Spanish in English-speaking societies* (pp. 33–55). Philadelphia: John Benjamin Publishing.

García, O., & Kleifgen, J.A. (2010). *Educating emergent bilinguals: Policies, programs, and practices for English language learners*. New York: Teacher's College Press.

Garret, J.E., & Holcomb, S. (2005). Meeting the needs of immigrant students with limited English ability. *International Education, 35*(1), 49–62.

Genesee, F. (2008). Early dual language learning. *Zero to Three, 29*(1), 17–23.

Goodwin, A.L. (2002). Teacher preparation and the education of immigrant children. *Education and Urban Society, 34*(2), 156–172. http://dx.doi.org/10.1177/0013124502034002003

Gray, P.B. & Young, S.M. (2011). Human-pet dynamics in cross cultural perspective. *Anthrozoos, 24*(1), 17–30.

Hakuta, K. (1978). A report on the development of grammatical morphemes in a Japanese girl learning English as a second language. In E.M. Hatch (Ed.), *Second language acquisition: A book of readings* (pp. 132–147). Rowley, MA: Newbury House Publishers.

Hardin, B., Lower, J., Robinson Smallwood, G., Chakravarthi, S., Li, L., & Jordan, C. (2010). Teachers, families, and communities supporting English language learners in inclusive pre-kindergarten: An evaluation of a professional development model. *Journal of Early Childhood Teacher Education, 31*(1), 20–36. http://dx.doi.org/10.1080/10901020903539580.

Haugen, E. (1972). *The ecology of language*. Stanford, CA: Stanford University Press.

Hold on to your home language. (2012). Toronto, ON: Ryerson University School of Early Childhood Education. Retrieved from http://www.ryerson.ca/mylanguage

Igoa, C. (1995). *The inner world of the immigrant child*. Mahwah, New Jersey: Lawrence Erlbaum Associates.

Itoh, H., & Hatch, E.M. (1978). Second language acquisition: A case study. In E.M. Hatch (Ed.), *Second language acquisition: A book of readings* (pp. 76–88). Rowley, MA: Newbury House Publishers.

Kagan, S.L., & Neuman, M.J. (1998). Lessons from three decades of transition research. *Elementary School Journal, 98*(4), 365–379. http://dx.doi.org/10.1086/461902

Kan, P.F., & Kohnert, K. (2005). Preschoolers learning Hmong and English: Lexical-semantic skills in L1 and L2. *Journal of Speech, Language, and Hearing Research: JSLHR, 48*(2), 372–383. http://dx.doi.org/10.1044/1092-4388(2005/026) Medline:15989399

Kenner, C. (2000). *Home pages: Literacy links for bilingual children*. Stoke-on-Trent, UK: Trentham Books.

Kirova, A. (2001). Loneliness in immigrant children: Implications for classroom practice. *Childhood Education, 77*(5), 260–267.

Kirova, A. (2003). Accessing children's experiences of loneliness through conversations. *Field Methods, 15*(1), 3–24. http://dx.doi.org/10.1177/1525822X02239572

Kohnert, K., Yim, D., Nett, K., Kan, P.F., & Duran, L. (2005). Intervention with linguistically diverse preschool children: A focus on developing home language(s). *Language, Speech, and Hearing Services in Schools, 36*(3), 251–263. http://dx.doi.org/10.1044/0161-1461(2005/025) Medline:16175888

Kovács, Á.M., & Mehler, J. (2009, April 21). Cognitive gains in 7-month-old bilingual infants. *Proceedings of the National Academy of Sciences of the United States of America, 106*(16), 6556–6560. http://dx.doi.org/10.1073/pnas.0811323106 Medline:19365071

Kraft-Sayre, M.E., & Pianta, R.C. (2000). *Enhancing the transition to kindergarten: Linking children, families, and schools.* Charlottesville, VA: University of Virginia, National Centre for Early Development and Learning.

Kramsch, C., & Steffensen, S.V. (2008). Ecological perspectives on second language acquisition and socialization. In P.A. Duff & N.H. Hornberger (Eds.), *Encyclopedia of language and education: Vol. 8. Language socialization* (2nd ed., pp. 17–28). Boston: Springer.

Krashen, S. (2004). *The power of reading: Insights from the research.* Portsmouth, NH: Heinemann.

Krashen, S., & Terrell, T. (1983). *The natural approach.* Hayward, CA: Alemany.

Kroll, J.F., Bobb, S.C., Misra, M., & Guo, T. (2008). Language selection in bilingual speech: Evidence for inhibitory processes. *Acta Psychologica, 128*(3), 416–430. http://dx.doi.org/10.1016/j.actpsy.2008.02.001 Medline:18358449

Kuhl, P.K. (2004). Early language acquisition: Cracking the speech code. *Nature Reviews: Neuroscience, 5*(11), 831–843. http://dx.doi.org/10.1038/nrn1533 Medline:15496861

Lambert, W.E. (1975). Culture and language as factors in learning and education. In A. Wolfgang (Ed.), *Education of immigrant students* (pp. 55–83). Toronto: Ontario Institute for Studies in Education.

Lawrence-Lightfoot, S. (2005). Reflections on portraiture: A dialogue between art and science. *Qualitative Inquiry, 11*(1), 3–14. http://dx.doi.org/10.1177/1077800404270955

Lawrence-Lightfoot, S., & Hoffman Davis, J. (1997). *The art and science of portraiture.* San Francisco, CA: Jossey-Bass.

Li, W., & Zhu, H. (2006). Development of code-switching and L1 attrition in L2 setting. *Birkbeck Studies in Applied Linguistics, 1,* 68–81.

Lucas, T., & Villegas, A.M. (2010). The missing piece in teacher education: The preparation of linguistically responsive teachers. *National Society for the Study of Education, 109*(2), 297–318.

Ma, J. (2004). *Reading the word and the world: A child in the interplay of her contexts in the reading of dual-language books with her mother tongue.* Unpublished doctoral dissertation, University of Bristol, UK.

Ma, J. (2008). "Reading the word and the world": How mind and culture are mediated through the use of dual-language storybooks. *Education, 36*(3), 237–251.

Mahon, M., Crutchley, A., & Quinn, T. (2003). New directions in the assessment of bilingual children. *Child Language Teaching and Therapy, 19*(3), 237–243. http://dx.doi.org/10.1191/0265659003ct253ed

Matthews, H. (2008). *Supporting a diverse and culturally competent workforce: Charting progress for babies in child care.* Washington, DC: Centre for Law and Social Policy. Retrieved from http://s242739747.onlinehome.us/publications/cp_rationale5.pdf

Matthews, H., & Ewen, D. (2010). *Early education programs and children of immigrants: Learning each other's language.* Washington, DC: Urban Institute. Retrieved from http://www.urban.org/publications/412205.html

McCain, M.N., Mustard, J.F., & McCuaig, K. (2011). *Early Years Study 3: Making decisions, taking action.* Toronto: Margaret & Wallace McCain Family Foundation. Retrieved from http://earlyyearsstudy.ca/

Moll, L.C., Amanti, C., Neff, D., & González, N. (1992). Funds of knowledge for teaching: Using a qualitative approach to connect homes and classrooms. *Theory into Practice, 31*(2), 132–141. http://dx.doi.org/10.1080/00405849209543534

National Association for Early Childhood Education. (2009). *Developmentally appropriate practice in early childhood programs serving children from birth through age eight.* Retrieved from http://www.naeyc.org/DAP

National Centre for Languages. (2006). *Positively Plurilingual.* London: Author. Retrieved from http://www.cilt.org.uk/home.aspx

Nemeth, K. (2009). *Many languages, one classroom: Teaching dual and English language learners.* Maryland: Gryphon House.

Olsen, L. (2000). Learning English and learning America: Immigrants in the center of a storm. *Theory into Practice, 39*(4), 196–202. http://dx.doi.org/10.1207/s15430421tip3904_2

Ontario Ministry of Children and Youth Services. (2007). *Early learning for every child today (ELECT): A framework for Ontario early childhood settings.* Toronto: Author. Retrieved from http://www.children.gov.on.ca/htdocs/English/topics/earlychildhood/early_learning_for_every_child_today.aspx

Ontario Ministry of Education. (2006). *Kindergarten program.* Toronto: Author. Retrieved from http://www.edu.gov.on.ca/eng/curriculum/elementary/kindergarten.html

Ontario Ministry of Education. (2007). *Supporting English language learners in kindergarten: A practical guide for Ontario educators.* Toronto: Author. Retrieved from http://www.edu.gov.on.ca/eng/document/kindergarten/kindergartenELL.pdf

Pacini-Ketchabaw, V. (2007). Child care and multiculturalism: A site of governance marked by flexibility and openness. *Contemporary Issues in Early Childhood, 8*(3), 222–232. http://dx.doi.org/10.2304/ciec.2007.8.3.222

Papademetriou, D.G., & Weidenfeld, W. (2007). *The children that Europe forgot.* Washington, DC: Transatlantic Task Force on Immigration and Integration. Retrieved from http://www.migrationpolicy.org/pubs/PapademetriouChildrenEuropeForgot09202007.pdf

Paradis, J., Genesee, F., & Crago, M.B. (2010). *Dual language development and disorders: A handbook on bilingualism and second language learning* (2nd ed.). Baltimore, MD: Brookes Publishing.

Patton, M.Q. (2002). *Qualitative research and evaluation methods* (3rd ed.). Thousand Oaks, CA: Sage.

Pelletier, J., Hipfner-Boucher, K., & Doyle, A. (2010). *Family literacy in action: A guide for literacy program facilitators.* Toronto: Scholastic Education.

Pelletier, J. (2011). School-based family literacy intervention programs. *Research for Teachers, 3.* Retrieved from http://www.etfo.ca/resources/researchforteachers/pages/default.aspx.

Poulin-Dubois, D., Blaye, A., Coutya, J., & Bialystok, E. (2011). The effects of bilingualism on toddlers' executive functioning. *Journal of Experimental Child Psychology, 108*(3), 567–579. http://dx.doi.org/10.1016/j.jecp.2010.10.009.

Quiroz, B., Snow, C., & Zhao, J. (2010). Vocabulary skills of Spanish-English bilinguals: Impact of mother-child language interactions and home language and literacy support. *International Journal of Bilingualism, 14*(3), 379–399. Retrieved from http://ijb.sagepub.com/content/14/4/379

Riches, C., & Genesee, F. (2006). Cross-linguistic and cross-modal aspects of literacy development. In F. Genesee, K. Lindholm-Leary, W. Saunders, & D. Christian (Eds.) *Educating English language learners: A synthesis of research evidence* (pp. 64–108). New York: Cambridge University Press.

Roche, D. (1999). *Can you greet the whole wide world? 12 common phrases in 12 different languages.* Boston: Houghton Mifflin.

Saville-Troike, M. (1988). Private speech: Evidence for second language learning strategies during the "silent" period. *Journal of Child Language, 15*(3), 567–590. http://dx.doi.org/10.1017/S0305000900012575 Medline:3198723

Schiff-Meyers, N.B. (1992). Considering arrested language development and language loss in the assessment of second language learners. *Language, Speech, and Hearing Services in Schools, 23,* 28–33.

Schoorman, D. (2001). Addressing the academic needs of immigrant students: Issues and trends in immigrant education. In C.F. Diaz (Ed.), *Multicultural education in the 21st century* (pp. 85–108). New York: Addison-Wesley.

Schwarzer, D., Haywood, A., & Lorenzen, C. (2003). Fostering multi-literacy in a linguistically diverse classroom: How does a monolingual teacher support linguistic diversity in a classroom of children who speak many different native languages? *Language Arts, 80*(6), 453–460.

Snow, C. (1997). Foreword. In P. Tabors (Ed.). *One child, two languages: A guide for preschool educators of children learning English as a second language* (pp. ix–xi). Baltimore: Brookes Publishing.

Snow, C., Burns, M.S., & Griffin, P. (1998). *Preventing reading difficulties in young children.* Washington, DC: National Academy.

Statistics Canada. (2006a). *Immigration and citizenship highlight tables, 2006 census.* Retrieved from http://www12.statcan.ca/census-recensement/2006/dp-pd/hlt/97-557/Index-eng.cfm.

Statistics Canada. (2006b). Population by mother tongue and age groups, 2006 counts, for Canada and census metropolitan areas and census agglomerations (table). *Language Table Highlights, 2006 Census* (Statistics Canada Catalogue No. 97-555-XWE2006002). Retrieved from http://www12.statcan.ca/census-recensement/2006/ref/rp-guides/lang-eng.cfm.

Stebih, I. (2003). Language minority children walk in two worlds. *Canadian Children,* *28,* 24–30.

Tabors, P. (1982). *Panos: A case study of a bilingual child.* Unpublished manuscript. Harvard Graduate School of Education, Cambridge, MA.

Tabors, P. (2008). *One child, two languages: A guide for early childhood educators of children learning English as a second language* (2nd ed.). Baltimore: Brookes Publishing.

Tabors, P., & Snow, C. (1994). English as a second language in preschools. In F. Genesee (Ed.), *Educating second language children: The whole child, the whole curriculum, the whole community* (pp. 103–125). New York: Cambridge University Press.

Tan, S. (2007). *The arrival.* New York: Scholastic.

Taylor, L., Bernhard, J.K., Garg, S., & Cummins, J. (2008). Affirming plural belonging: Building on students' family-based cultural and linguistic capital through multiliteracies pedagogy. *Journal of Early Childhood Literacy, 8*(3), 269–295. http://dx.doi.org/10.1177/1468798408096481

Thompson, L. (2000). *Young bilingual learners in nursery school.* Clevedon, UK: Multilingual Matters.

Titon, J.T. (Ed.). (2009). *Worlds of music: An introduction to the music of the world's peoples* (3rd ed.). Belmont, CA: Schirmer Cengage Learning.

U.S. Census Bureau. (2000). *2000 census of population and housing.* Retrieved from http://www.census.gov/prod/cen2000/

Wei, L. (2011). Moment analysis and translanguaging space: Discursive construction of identities by multilingual Chinese youth in Britain. *Journal of Pragmatics, 43*(5), 1222–1235. http://dx.doi.org/10.1016/j.pragma.2010.07.035

Wolf, K. (2002). *Reflection model: The reflective practitioner.* Retrieved from http://sites.google.com/site/reflection4learning/teachers/nc-reflection-model

Wong Fillmore, L. (1991). When learning a second language means losing the first. *Early Childhood Education Quarterly, 6,* 323–346.

Wong Fillmore, L. (2000). Loss of family languages: Should educators be concerned? *Theory into Practice, 39*(4), 203–210. http://dx.doi.org/10.1207/s15430421tip3904_3

Woods, P., Boyle, M., & Hubbard, N. (1999). *Multicultural children in the early years: Creative teaching, meaningful learning.* Clevedon, UK: Multilingual Matters.

Yngve, V. (1996). *From grammar to science: New foundations for general linguistics.* Philadelphia: John Benjamins.

Young Children. (2001–2010). Washington, DC: National Association for the Education of Young Children (NAEYC).

Zhang, J. (2009). *Implementation and evaluation of a Chinese language family literacy program: Impact on young children's literacy development in English and Chinese.* Unpublished doctoral dissertation, Ontario Institute for Studies in Education, University of Toronto, Toronto, ON.

Zigler, E., & Kagan, S.L. (1982). Child development knowledge and educational practice: Using what we know. In A. Lieberman & M. McLaughlin (Eds.), *Policy making in education* (pp. 80–104). Chicago: University of Chicago Press.

INDEX